MEN, WOMEN & ME

To my mother,
and all the friends who know who they are,
especially H, Philip and Joan

Marcelle d'Argy Smith

MEN,
WOMEN
& ME

Ebury Press London

Published by Ebury Press
Division of The National Magazine Company Ltd.
Colquhoun House, 27-37 Broadwick Street,
London WIV 1FR

First impression 1987

ISBN 0 85223 633 6

Designed by Gwyn Lewis

Computerset in Great Britain by
MFK Typesetting Ltd., Hitchin, Herts.
Printed and bound in Great Britain at
the Bath Press, Avon.

Contents

Introduction

$\mathcal{I}$ don't know why I started writing. Or maybe I do. Deirdre McSharry, the then Editor of *Cosmopolitan*, used to stop me by the lift sometimes as we worked in the same building. She used to say in that persuasive voice of hers 'Oh I do wish you'd write for us', and I'd say I was too busy living. It was a smart-arsed line that I've probably read somewhere, but there was some truth to it. In those days I was the publisher of two annuals about art and antiques and I spent nearly three months of each year travelling abroad. Plus my personal life was lived at a fairly intense pace. By my thirties I was into heavy negotiations with men. Trying to explain, trying to communicate, trying to get across the female point of view, striving for a *real* understanding. You know how it is. Of course the other thing was, I didn't know how to write. I didn't know what you were supposed to say and how you were supposed to say it, and what sort of mysterious intelligence it took to sit down and write 'an article'.

I was rather in awe of all journalists and writers. They obviously *knew* more than I did. They knew about sitting down in front of a typewriter and coming up with a beginning, a middle and an end to a piece. I grasped the general concept, but I didn't really know how they did it. And there was no-one to ask. You just *do* it was all anyone said. Look, in those days I didn't realise that sitting down in front of a typewriter was maybe the hardest part. But I suppose I was flattered that the Editor of *Cosmopolitan* thought I had anything to *say* that could possibly be of interest to anyone. It is true that I was beginning to have the urge to scribble down for myself some of the things that were happening around me, to friends of mine, to people I knew and met. I kept thinking there had to be some *sense* to be made of it all.

In my teens I'd started writing 'rhymes'. You couldn't call them poems. Sometimes, if I felt bold, I'd give them to the people they were written about. The telephone operator at the Institute of Directors where I worked as a secretary was much nicer to me when I apologised with a rhyme. A tall gangly blond man on whom I had the most enormous crush was more, well, responsive, in an off-hand way when I sent him some writing in rhyme. We did, at least, become friends. I suppose it was a way of getting through to people and it absorbed me and made me laugh. Then I forgot about it. I moved to London and shared a flat in Dolphin Square with three very ambitious, very attractive women who talked about men constantly. They didn't talk *to* men that much as I recall. They all wanted to get married. I wanted to fall in love. I wanted to *feel* something other than social approval. There was an ad in the personal column of *The Times* one day in the January of my twenty-second year. It said, 'Secretary for Côte d'Azur, Fluent French. Car driver.' After a couple of false starts I got the job. A long black limousine with masses of fragrant mimosa in the back window picked me up at Nice Airport on a brilliant blue sky day in February.

I remember the drive along the Moyenne Corniche to the Château Balzan past all the little villages on the way to Eze. Once I'd spent four weeks when I was seventeen at Cap d'Ail at a French summer school and I'd loved it. Those warm days and warm evenings and the scent of pine needles had stayed in my memory and I'd vowed to come back. But I'd almost forgotten until now. The French language had always pleasured me. I found I became a different person when I spoke a different language. And there was the sun, the Mediterranean heat and romance of the Côte d'Azur. Robert Graves had said that the South of France was like a whore with a glamorous presence, a shady past and an uncertain future. It was the territory of Scott Fitzgerald and the Murphys, Picasso, Chagall. Maybe this time I'd get to Plage de la Garoupe and sit where they'd all sat in the 'Twenties when the sun wasn't fashionable. I suppose that France seemed to me then to be about intellectual conversation and intense brown haired men who smoked dark tobacco.

I stayed in the job for two extraordinary months. There was little to do except send off the odd telex to New York, speak to the staff, plan menus and help entertain the constant stream of rich, famous and international guests who came to dine. In some ways I enjoyed the private isolation, because despite the company I was very alone with my thoughts. It was fascinating watching people communicate. Or not communicate. The sumptuous sit-down dinners for twenty often produced witty conversations that were about business or Monte Carlo gossip. Rarely were they personal. My American employer was old and had divorced four wives. He was immensely wily and manipulative. But what struck me was because he was enormously rich the people around him *let* him manipulate them, particularly the women. When I spoke to people on a one-to-one basis they were rarely as sparkling or happy as they appeared. Lots of people had to wait until *Dallas* or *Dynasty* to understand that 'money don't buy you love' although it can buy you good scenery and props. I was rather grateful to know that at twenty-two.

I left and moved to Nice because I couldn't face the thought of London and the rain. Not just then. I'd saved a bit of money and I promised my mother I'd be home just as soon as the money ran out. She called it wasting time, but I wasn't so sure. I moved into the cheapest hotel I could find in Avenue Gambetta. It had an 1890's feel about it what with the wrought iron railings and the cornices on the high ceilings. It was suddenly wonderful to be alone, to be free, to be away from the surfeit of grandeur. Each day I went to the beach with my battered paperback copies of Henry Miller and Simone de Beauvoir and Scott Fitzgerald. For two weeks I didn't speak to anyone except the concierge, Ella, who wished me good morning and good evening each day. On the third week I met Robert when his dog bounced onto my blue and white beach mattress and refused to leave. Robert became my first love affair and I stayed in France for the next nine months.

I did love him. He was vital and teeming with energy and he rode wild horses when we went to the Camargue for a few days. He was funny with a deep throaty chuckle and he had marvellous laugh lines at the corners of his green eyes and he said he could never be bothered with foreign women because they couldn't speak French properly. 'You can say everything you *need* to say but not everything you *want* to say,' he said. So my French really *did* become fluent. I stayed on at the small hotel and saw him practically every day. His friends ranged from Jean-Luc who worked on *Paris Match* to François, a surgeon at Nice Hospital, to Charlot the local butcher. Sometimes when I was with him racing in the car to Antibes or exploring Biot or eating at Saint Paul de Vence, just he and I talking endlessly together, I couldn't believe I'd spent so long in the stifled atmosphere at the Château. Well, it was all right as a learning experience. But I wondered how other people wanted to *live* that sort of life when there was this sort of intimacy and warmth on offer. We did discuss me getting another job so as I could stay 'sur la côte' and I remember one sultry afternoon auditioning to be a dancer while Robert waited for me in the car outside in one of the side streets in Juan-les-Pins. I was offered the job, start in the back row and let's see how you do, but as you had to tour throughout France with the dance company there didn't seem much point. I was wearing a square cut rather revealing dress in brown, tangerine and green stripes and Robert hugged me as I hopped back into the small open car. 'I'd have hired you,' he said to me. 'I'd definitely have hired you.' And we drove to a restaurant near the beach and he teased me over Campari and orange about what sort of dancer I'd have been and how he could have spent his evenings following the dance troupe around and waiting for me at stage doors. We got rather drunk in the sun as I recall.

It was a poignant first affair, played out against a fantasy backdrop. I couldn't have wished for a better man or a better place. But I didn't know what you *did* with love. If you didn't want to get married you had to say goodbye. Not that we discussed marriage or even love that summer. We didn't do that until twelve years later when we were sitting in a small restaurant in Haut-de-Cagnes one evening and we both said how we'd felt about each other. When I came back to London in the late autumn of my twenty-second year the wedding race was on.

Within two years most of my friends had rushed down aisles and into marriages. I couldn't understand it. What were they *doing* when there was a whole life out there just waiting to be lived? Don't ask me why I didn't associate 'marriage' with 'life'. I just didn't. I thought it was closer to death. It was so final. The end. You couldn't see other people, except on a rather formal basis, you could never again meet someone and think I'd like to get to *know* this person. You couldn't even see your friends except at tight little dinners for couples or possibly over a snatched working lunch. Everyone approached it with such *gravity*. It was a *very* serious business and enjoying yourself didn't come into it. Marriage was *not* about having fun. Heavens no. What struck me most in my early twenties was that most people who did it didn't even appear to be wildly in love. Women mostly married for security, men who'd been around for a while with women they 'fancied', then settled for someone 'suitable', rich friends merely amalgamated, some people married absolutely anybody willing to go through the ceremony with them, some drifted into it because their relationships were getting rather stale and they thought that marriage might be the answer, and others said they didn't want to be lonely when they got old.

There were few instances of terrific friendship and any depth of understanding. There was little evidence of passion, of any real emotion on either side. I wanted some of that before I dropped dead for Chrissakes. I remembered Robert had said to me 'One day, when you do marry, make sure you really *love* him. Make sure he's the sort of person you want to talk to over breakfast in the morning. Make sure you *care*.' So yes, I cried at weddings, very regularly. I cried for men who didn't understand and women who thought it was going to be okay. And I cried for myself because I was losing friends and I was at a loss to explain what my mother called my cynical point of view. 'I can't understand why you don't want a normal life,' she said. 'But they're not even going to be *happy*,' I moaned. And she said what did I know and exactly how happy was I going to be? One or two of them survived. The tall gangly blond I'd liked in my teens said years later, 'Why didn't you stop me? You *saw* what I was doing. I wasted, completely wasted six years of my life.' 'But it might *not* have been a mistake,' I said.

I'm not anti-marriage. It's just that some of the people who do it give it a bad name. It was probably in those days of my early twenties that I became fascinated by 'relationships'. What people did and why and for how long and what they felt and what the consequence was. God knows I was busy trying to work out my own salvation, trying to live and learn

5

and get it right one day. Listen, I honestly thought that 'one day' you did magically get life right. I had single friends like me who were striding through life talking about 'never compromising'. We were waiting for the Biggie, that special, unique, unbearably wonderful person who would appear with a kind of divine light around them so we'd *know* unquestionably that this was The One.

Someone said to me recently 'Relationships is such a 'Seventies sort of word'. Yep, I guess it is. Much as Togetherness was a 'Fifties word and 'Sex' was a 'Sixties word. God knows what the buzzword for the 'Eighties is. It's probably 'Work' or 'Unemployment' or 'AIDS' or 'Apartheid' or 'Filofax' or 'Third World' or 'Rape' or 'Property' or 'Nuclear Free Zone'. 'Who's interested in bloody *relationships*?' a man friend said. As he's been divorced twice and falls in love with the regularity of Big Ben striking, I didn't think it worth replying. The truth is we're *all* interested even though to admit it may no longer be fashionable. There may be broader issues at stake, but they're not necessarily *more* important. Most people I know, married, single and divorced, are still struggling, still hoping to get it right. They have been for as long as I've known them.

About six years ago one of my closest friends who'd been living with a man for about six years suddenly became pregnant. I loved them both and thought they had a tricky but on the whole rather good thing going. The man went berserk, and said that he didn't want more children and after all he was still married – to the wife he'd left seven years previously. They parted for a week but he said he missed her. He didn't know where anything was and he couldn't find his socks in the morning. And he couldn't understand why if she really *loved* him she wouldn't have an abortion. *She* said I do love him but I've always wanted children and I always meant to have them and if he really loved *me* he'd understand. Well, on one hand it was funny stuff, on the other hand there were two people suffering terribly. Two people I loved who loved each other. Finally the man got divorced from the wife he'd left seven years pre-viously and after various grumbles and displays of bad temper during the pregnancy he began to get terribly excited about it all. He attended the birth and was thrilled to bits. They married a year later. Today they have

6

a most successful marriage and another child. I decided when they married that I didn't understand *anything*. It's all very well asking wearily what do *women* want? What do *men* want? Does *anybody* know what they want? Or do they have to wait until things are thrust upon them? At about that time I sat down and wrote a rhyme for myself called 'Plea to Scott' which was all about the couple who'd married when their child was a year old. I wanted men to be as romantic and loving as Scott Fitzgerald seemed to have been in his day. The 'Eighties way of love and marriage was filling me with a quiet despair. It's a sad rhyme although it does make a point. I gave it to the woman friend who had the grace to smile. She said she supposed it was interesting to be written about. 'What if it got published?' I said. 'I don't mind,' she said. 'I can live with it.' And so I took it up to *Cosmopolitan* and it appeared a few months later. It was odd to see my scribbles in print. It occurred to me that I rather liked the feeling. Even the cynical sad thoughts put me in a good mood. I enjoyed playing with the words and there was a discipline attached to writing rhymes that appealed to me. It became a new hobby. Suddenly I wanted to comment on everything around me. A 'phone call would trigger off a wild bit of creativity. An evening with a difficult lover would make me want to come home and capture the mood on paper. A talk with a woman-friend would leave me dying to find a pen and any old piece of paper so I could record the moment. *Cosmopolitan* bought all the rhymes. But one thing was beginning to worry me. Say they weren't any good? Say they could be a whole lot better. Why wasn't anyone *criticising* me?

At that time there were other things to worry about. I'd been transferred to a deeply prestigious magazine about art and antiques and it was losing a great deal of money. For a few months I was meant to be 'running it' whatever that meant. It meant almost daily confrontations with the Managing Director, an associate publisher leaving because he couldn't bear to work for a woman and the almost certain knowledge that the magazine would be transferred to the USA by the end of the year. My love life was a shambles. The two men who'd been the most important in my life were otherwise engaged. One was living with an accommodating heiress, the other was insisting he wanted to be 'alone'.

Perhaps I was 'saved' at the time by a third. A sort of 'elastoplast' man because I was feeling very wounded. I'd known him when I was twenty-five and we'd stayed in touch in an absent-minded sort of way. I liked the odd 'phone calls. I probably needed them desperately to tell me I was still worth talking to. The only funny plus side to that year was that I was getting some feedback from the rhymes. I hadn't reckoned on that. They were my comments for me, maybe for my friends if they read them. But people I didn't know suddenly started saying, 'Oh I so identified with what you said', or 'You did make me laugh,' and people who read *Cosmopolitan* started writing to me. I was getting rhymes *back* from men.

When redundancy came along with a fat cheque I knew exactly what I wanted to do. Screw the recession, screw unemployment, screw absolutely everybody. I wanted to learn to *write*. And I wanted to live in New York. I'd been there masses of times but I wanted to abandon myself to the city in much the same way as I'd done to the South of France years before. I wanted a 'plane ticket with no return date on it. I also wanted to be a student. That's the thing about staying single. Sometimes you get to do exactly what you want.

Jackie helped me pack and Jo and Annette said they'd write and Paul said he was envious and H said he hoped I knew what I was doing and Selwyn said it was marvellous and Ann and John said we're thrilled for you and Joan and Philip said they'd love to have me come and stay with them on Central Park West and Johnnie said he'd come and see me and *Cosmopolitan* sent me a Good Luck telegram and my mother said you're *not* going to New York whatever *for?*

I dashed off a quick rhyme to Joan that first night in New York – I was so *ecstatic* to be there, to be *living* there. It was like being in love. Well I was in love again. But this time with a city. I sensed then it would be almost impossible to leave and I remember talking to New York as if it were a person that night in my bedroom. I had the feeling that it might be my most tumultuous love affair ever. It was all dramatic, romantic stuff but in a way I wasn't too far wrong.

A couple of days later I caught the M104 bus that trundled up Broadway to 114th street and Columbia University and enrolled in my first writing workshop. Well, it wasn't quite as simple as that. Enrolling took most of a day. It was such a complicated business what with all the forms you had to fill in and the different buildings on campus you had to visit. My first class was with a wonderfully funny woman who looked like Anne Bancroft and sounded like all those urgent warm New Yorkers you saw in films. She stared around the room and said 'I'm *not* taking all of you. There's twenty-eight people here and the maximum for a workshop is fourteen people. Anyone who hasn't shown me a piece of written work that's any good by next week will have to leave.' God. Oh God. Nobody had told me you had to write *before* you were accepted. I hadn't written anything except those rhymes since I was seventeen. I crept into Butler library the following day and began the torturous task of writing something. I didn't know what to write about so I wrote about London. I didn't know if it was good or bad or dreadful or so-so or silly or okay. That night I posted it to Phyllis Raphael, the Anne Bancroft look-alike, with a terse note. It said I thought she ought to *know* that I'd left my job and my apartment and my life and my country to come to New York to learn to write. And at least someone at Columbia ought to have *said* it was not possible when I'd phoned a couple of months ago. I *had* phoned. She accepted me in her 'creative non-fiction class' and I enrolled in another class with a wonderful-sounding name – 'Structure and Style'. Phyllis frequently said that writing and life had great parallels and I certainly yearned for structure and style in *my* life. Phyllis was gutsy and when I got to know her later on a personal basis, when I'd stopped behaving like an awe-struck student, she talked honestly about love and marriage and men. And disappointment. Glenda Adams who ran the other class was a gentle Australian who'd been at Sydney University with Clive James. Both were clever and polished writers who'd published books and took their craft very seriously. I *loved* being a student. Gradually the workshops became alive and vivid as I got to know the other writers. I began to realise that the pieces of writing that held my attention were the *honest* pieces, the owning-up pieces, the writing about *relationships*. It was hard to write about yourself. Say no-one wanted to listen? Say you looked completely foolish? Say no-one was *interested*? At the beginning I thought it was like stripping off and showing everyone your tits and risking them laughing. The fourteen of us edged warily into our revelations, we were unsure of our perceptions, we were uneasy with our audience. But we became bolder and dared to say things. Yes, we criticised each other. But it was heartfelt and constructive and we learned and learned. Having left London and the fractious love affairs I was free to write about them. I could see things better from a distance and writing helped me analyse. When you write you're forced to think about what you're writing and suddenly for the first time a lot of things I hadn't understood fell into place. I found I could describe thoughts and emotions and remember dialogue. No one laughed at me except when they were meant to. My class mates used to listen earnestly and say 'But what happened next?'

Being with a crowd of New Yorkers who were so direct and encouraging really helped through the agonising business of finding my own 'voice' and daring to express myself. Also daring to say 'I'. For ages I couldn't do that and I'd hide behind the third person. What also came home to me with a resounding blow was that I couldn't *invent* stories. I remember Phyllis saying, 'The truth is such a straitjacket when you're writing. Use your *imagination*.' The truth was that my mind couldn't possibly *imagine* anything more fascinating than what was really happening to me and the people I knew. Glenda said, 'Good God are these *real* names?' and I said, 'Yes, they help me to remember better.' I don't know why my friends have never minded being written about. But no-one, with the exception of H, has ever complained. He said did I have to be so personal? And the answer is yes I do. I suppose because I want 'the truth' I'm determined to write it – more or less. Of course I've learned to edit things in my brain these days and yes I've learned to be a *bit* creative. That year at Columbia, those privileged hours in the writing workshops, gave me a respect for writing and good writers and a glimpse into how difficult a craft it is to perfect. I don't write. Maybe I've learned to communicate and for that I'm grateful.

I never knew how I was going to leave New York. Sometimes in a masochistic mood I'd pull out my suitcases and pretend that today was the day and I'd mentally rehearse the packing and the goodbyes and the cab ride through the streets to the airport. And how I'd be thinking when the 'plane took off above my favourite city. When it all became too dreadful to contemplate I'd run the mental picture in reverse and pretend I was coming back again and I'd ask the yellow-cab driver to stop on the Triboro' bridge so I could gaze out across Manhattan. Probably I never would have come to the decision to leave. I used to think that I'd have procrastinated until every last bit of money had run out and my friends had long since stopped feeding me and washed their hands of me and I'd have ended up alone and forgotten, a bag-lady in Central Park. There never would have been a right time to go. I kept remembering that song with the words like, 'If ever I could leave you it wouldn't be in springtime, summer, winter or fall.' A fiendishly bright black woman in one of my writing workshops had said to me, 'I understand how you feel the way you do about men and women but how the hell can you feel so Goddamned emotional about this *city*? It's just a place for Chrissakes.' And I said I didn't know I just did.

One Friday evening in the March of 1983 I was dancing wildly at New York University to a terrific rock group called 'Urban Blight'. By eight o'clock the next morning I was lying in intensive care in St. Vincent's Hospital in Greenwich Village. There was a pacemaker strapped to an artery in my right thigh. Cardiac arrest they said. I'd dimly remembered the scene in the crowded bar at Number One Fifth Avenue where we'd gone for a nightcap and I'd suddenly felt faint. A tall good-looking blond man had smiled at me across the room and it was he who caught me as I fell to the floor. He held me in his arms under the canopy outside the restaurant door while Marta, Jim and a frantic waiter rushed into the street to try and attract the attention of a taxi. The rain was lashing across the sidewalks, Marta was yelling and the waiter finally almost hurled himself on to the bonnet of a cab and said, 'You've *got* to stop.' The cab ride is a blurred memory of being sick and feeling floaty and no pain and the tall man saying, 'I don't like the look of her, we've got to get her to hospital.' I couldn't speak. I didn't know where words came from. But I could hear and dimly understand. They rushed me through a rubbery side door of St. Vincent's – 'Christ we should really take her to Lenox Hill,' Marta said, and Steve, the tall blond man, had replied it was too far,

11

too dangerous to risk it.

I remember being laid on a stretcher trolley and a doctor rolling up my sleeve and inserting a needle. And I started to close my eyes because I was weary and the pandemonium in the Casualty department was all too solid and real and I was beginning to float. In my mind the stretcher trolley started to race down a long grey corridor with dark grey cabinets stacked up on either side and at the end of the tunnel I could see a circle of bright white light, 'This is *ridiculous*,' I thought, 'I'm dying.' When I came round in a small side ward opposite an attemped suicide, a pregnant woman with a slashed throat and a man who said he thought his liver had fallen out Marta was smiling at me. 'Cor, I thought things were going to turn ugly,' I said.

Two doctors who really were called Cohen and Murphy said, 'We're going to have to take you in to Coronary Care.' Well, I thought, it's the weekend. The rest of the hospital is probably full. It didn't occur to me there was anything wrong with my heart. On the Saturday morning as I lay on my bed by the window I stared out at the New York sky and said to God, 'All right, okay you win, I'm going home.' I remember thinking it was a relief that the decision had been taken out of my hands. Joan crept into see me on that morning and sat thoughtfully by my bedside. 'You look terrible Marce,' she said. 'When I heard the news I kept thinking about that poem "Death Wishes" where you'd said you wanted to die in New York.' 'I *nearly* made it Joan,' I said. 'Number One Fifth Avenue sounds pretty good to me.' Joan said would I mind awfully dying somewhere else at some other time because frankly it was all too much for her to cope with on a lousy weekend when she was cooking for ten. 'I can't bear this,' she said. 'You'd better get well really soon.' For the next few days and in the weeks that followed everyone was wonderful to me.

Six weeks later, Joan, Katharine and I boarded a British Airways flight to London and I didn't feel a thing. Not a thing. Except life was rather funny after all.

It was odd to be home again. I'd changed. I remembered what Scott Fitzgerald had said about becoming a different person and the different person wanting different things. A lot had happened to other people.

Two friends had had cancer, Fiona had committed suicide, someone I loved a lot had had a heart attack, five people had moved – they all said property values were skyrocketing and did I realise how much money they'd made. Jo's kid brother had died, *everyone* was talking about how hard they were working and most people were still having trouble with their relationships. It's what living in the 'Eighties or probably any other time is all about.

Cosmopolitan asked me to write for them after I'd been home about six months. I wrote something about sex. Something flippant and cute that raised a smile then but would be deemed obscene and irresponsible today. We all feel differently about lots of things. Then I wrote a piece called 'Whoops I'm single!' Well, it was pretty honest. Being single, despite everything had been terrific as far as I was concerned, and even at the moment in hospital when I thought I only had ten minutes to *live* I realised I didn't have any regrets. Now Columbia had taught me how to write a beginning, a middle and an end and had given me courage I didn't mind at all sharing thoughts and odd jumbled bits of philosophy. If it struck a chord with someone, well and good. If not, I guessed they could turn the page.

It's good and bad, easy and difficult to write for *Cosmopolitan*. On one level it's very restricting knowing all the time that you're aiming at a readership that has a median age of twenty-five years. You can't be too cynical, clever, weary or say falling in love *isn't* wonderful necessarily, except when it is. You can't say take risks, get out there, live, life gets even better as you get older. People of twenty-five want to know about being in their twenties. Yet I find that restricting though it is, the *Cosmopolitan* readership today seems to be more responsive and aware and mature than I ever remember being. They're political and passionate. I'm touched by the way they empathise and so I go on writing for them. Once when I wrote an article about rejection I was thinking I can't really write this, who wants to *know*? Yet when the piece was published hundreds of people wrote in, women of all ages and quite a few men. One woman friend asked me how much longer I was going to go on writing like a breathless twenty-eight-year-old. God, I don't know. Twenty-eight year olds, thirty-eight year olds, forty-eight year olds and eighteen year olds all feel the same about *some* things. What's being a grown-up? Probably it's about understanding and accepting what happens to you and not expecting too much. I know very few grown-ups. Most of us are very mature and wise when things are going well for us.

Nearly all the following pieces have appeared in *Cosmopolitan* during the last three years. Some of them are articles I wanted to write and some of them are things I was asked to write. They're not meant to be meaningful. They were just life as I saw it at the time. If I get through to you, if the pieces mean anything to you, I'm thrilled. It means there's a person out there who's on the same wavelength and that makes me feel better. If not, well maybe you can give the book to someone else, someone like me who's still wobbling through.

Marcelle d'Argy Smith
London, October 1987

Men

My funny Valentine

Give me funny men. When all is said and done and it has been lately, they are the most attractive men in the world. And magically, funny doesn't fade. Most other attractions seem to, haven't you noticed? OK, I'm not talking Paul Newman's looks, because the man's a freak, a one-off. His wife Joanne Woodward reckons he's never had an ugly day in his life. It's just possible that I'd have looked for laughs elsewhere if I could have spent life with Paul. But he was always busy and he lives there and I live here and you know how it is. Robert Redford is no longer the man I sighed for in *The Way We Were*. The way he was was mouth-watering, but those blond college boy looks are not wearing too well and I'm noticing.

You can keep your Richard Geres, Pierce Brosnans, Christopher Lamberts and anyone else who looks like Dex Dexter in *Dynasty*. I find I'm watching them *very* critically for signs of physical deterioration. You think this sounds like male sexist patter coming from a woman? Well, physically attractive is what they're selling and physically attractive is what I'm buying when I watch them. When they're no longer a feast for my sexual eyes I'm disappointed.

But I do *notice* that Walter Matthau, a man with whom I would have *eloped*, is probably sagging and sixty. Do I *care* that Woody Allen has the physique of a ball-point pen and is losing tufts of hair as we speak? Do I *mind* if Clive James is smugly overweight and Jonathan Miller and John Cleese are into greying middle age? I couldn't care less. The more I see them, the more I adore them. Sometimes after watching a crack-you-up sketch with Ronnie Barker I sit back and think well I could have married *him*. Don't say but you couldn't imagine going to bed with him. He's not selling sex. He wants to make you laugh. But just imagine he

My funny Valentine

was the right sort of age and you knew him and you *did* go to bed with him. You'd probably be hooked. Listen, I think I might have been.

And would I have married Woody Allen? Yes, yes and yes, and for as long as it lasted I'd have been thrilled. I *know* he's neurotic but at least he's honest about it. And that nutty deeply perceptive humour of his makes life possible. He said the chief trouble with his marriage was that he put his wife under a pedestal, but who's heard Diane and Mia complaining?

For many years I've had an on/off ... er ... liaison with a funny man. Currently it's off, but who knows? In the insecure early days it wasn't the thought of him taking out other women, or indeed staying in with them, that worried me. And it wasn't sexual jealousy. What really pained me was a mental picutre of him *laughing* with someone else. I couldn't find another man to do that with. God knows I tried burying myself in sex and intense conversation with another person and you can do that and it's wonderful for a while. But then one day you find yourself looking at your new love object doing one of his endless office reports and you're thinking if it wasn't for sex I'd be bored. Then I'd think about the funny man and miss him. Of course I'm eccentric and he is difficult and together we're impossible. But he's a devastatingly hard act to follow.

The best thing about being with a funny man is that because there is humour sprinkled liberally across life, you can't taste the bad bits. You feel so relaxed and comfortable. He seems to have the answer to living. The worst thing is that everybody else who knows him feels exactly the same way about him and you can feel pretty damned selfish trying to spend time alone with him. Funny men do get invited out all the time. Well this one did and does and no doubt will till the day he dies. I'd underestimated the power of funny before I knew him. We used to eat at the same restaurant and I only noticed him because there were always a lot of people around his table. But he wasn't my type. I was mad about good looks then and embroiled with an American musician who was into heavy rock, and getting to know the right people in case he ever wrote a hit tune. Listen, it wasn't because he didn't write the hit tune but one day after I'd been mentally unfaithful over a couple of lunches with

My funny Valentine

the overweight, funny man with the slept-in face, I ceased to care about the musician. Well, I ceased to care enough. Suddenly I was being fascinated by a gentle, mumbling, half-cockney accent and suddenly I was laughing at *lunchtime*. It didn't really matter what this man looked like. Even now I have to concentrate to remember his imperfections. All I saw was a six-foot man with the grinniest green eyes and rather nice hands and yes, he did dress rather well, but that was more for business than any real pleasure. Of course he *could* be serious but mostly he didn't take life too personally. It didn't pay he said. He insisted that happiness was something he experienced in between long bouts of pain yet he was cheerful on a daily basis. He didn't chat me up, but he grew on me. Like a wart he said. When you meet him you don't think, 'I'd like to go to bed with you.' You tend to think, 'I'd like to stay awake with you as long as possible in case I miss something.' I should add that he has the imagination to be kind as well as funny. A fairly lethal combination when I came to think about it. I didn't for ages. About a year. And then one day he came to my apartment for a drink and he looked like a spaniel who'd been run over. Life was going wrong he said. For once he couldn't think of a funny solution. So I suggested the absurdest thing I could think of. 'How about,' I said, 'you and me going to bed together?' He looked puzzled but he did at least smile. 'Could be a bit of a rush job,' he said. 'I've only got half an hour.' But he did say, by now with a very *broad* smile, that it would probably make him feel better. And the funniest thing is it was lovely. Sort of Don Juan and Rupert Bear rolled into one and he went home whistling. I'd never felt so post-coitally secure in my life.

The following day he said let's go away for a weekend. He knew a couple with a cottage. We went to stay in Sussex with two people who were spending *their* first weekend away together. They weren't quite as relaxed with each other and they were both trying hard to do and say the right things. This was understandable but particularly tough on the girl who was suffering from a rather difficult stomach complaint. Every so often she'd have to disappear from the room to break wind. I *know* farting isn't particularly funny and its one of those bodily functions we all do and no one ever talks about because it's regarded as lavatory

My funny Valentine

humour. I *know* all that. But *you* try sleeping with a funny man when your night is punctuated by the sound of giant raspberries being blown in the next bedroom.

I don't honestly remember our sex life that weekend. All I can recall is tears of laughter and getting stomach cramps myself at his comments that accompanied each fresh windy outburst from the room next door. But I do remember thinking that desperate, smothered giggling combined with sticky togetherness is the *ultimate* in intimacy. One of my all-time best nights what with one thing and another. Next morning we were bleary-eyed and still trying not to smile too much. As he said, the main thing is to behave as though we hadn't heard a *thing* because there was male ego and female pride at stake here. Some people take their first nights together very seriously he said. It can't have been easy for them. And if we so much as *mention* the previous night we might ruin everything.

But as he was a master of the *double entendre* I kept spluttering through Sunday morning and there was a terrible quarter of an hour during the roast lamb and roast potatoes when I simply couldn't eat for silent, shaking, helpless laughter. And *he* started to chuckle because laughter is so bloody infectious. By Sunday evening the couple said hadn't it been the *most* wonderful time and we really ought to do it again. My funny man said gravely that it was probably impossible to repeat such a weekend.

As time went by and we started living together I did suggest he should try to lose weight but to no avail. He was always insisting he was going to start his diet on Monday. He said it regularly for seven years. He explained that the *real* problem was that for his age and weight he was too short. Once when I was browsing in Hatchards in Piccadilly, I came across a book called *How to Improve your Man in Bed*. There was a chapter on what to do if he is overweight. Most men have no conception of what you're talking about when you suggest that it's uncomfortable and even hard to breathe when you're making love with a heavy man. They need a visual image of you struggling under another weighty object. For instance, you could ask your man what he'd do if he came home and found the wardrobe on top of you. The man would obviously

My funny Valentine

say, 'That would be terrible. You'd be half crushed to death under that weight.' Then *you* could say, 'Hasn't it ever occurred to you that you probably weigh as much as the wardrobe?' It was all very simple, the book said. The man would obviously get the message and go on a diet and you'd live happily ever after. OK, so it's obviously an old book but the cute psychology appealed to me and I decided to try.

'What would you do if you came home and found me *pinned* down on the bed with the wardrobe on top of me?' I said one evening. He scratched his head. 'I'd be bloody amazed Marce,' he said. '*Why*?' I said. He smiled. 'Because you've got fitted cupboards here Marce. That's why.' I threw the sodding book away and he continued eating meals between snacks. It's true that sometimes he did start his diet and lose weight but always during the weeks we weren't seeing each other. I used to get reports back from friends saying he looked *great* now but he was pining for me.

You know when you've loved a man who whistles to himself, can make you laugh when you've been stung on the lip by a wasp and who can manage to be funny when you've given him two sleeping pills instead of aspirin, he's hard to replace. A funny man gets into your bloodstream like malaria. Sometimes you feel sick to the gills wondering whether you'll ever find such humour again. Other men don't have that rare perception and outlook on life. Other men are more self-absorbed and less aware of the absurdity of one's everyday existence. Other men are repressed by comparison. Oh I've met men who laugh at *me* and men who are desperate tellers of jokes. But heaven save me from people who are so bad at real communication they feel they have to tell you *jokes*.

The truth is in my part of the world there's an alarming shortage of men confident enough and wise enough to be funny. My friend Jeffrey is a sort of substitute and even though he's married, his wife does let us laugh together sometimes. I'm grateful for that. Sometimes we chortle as a threesome and I like that, too. Mind you, last week I did have dinner with a short, thin Woody Allenish man whose wife had run off with an actor. The night we dined his dog was dying. He said he was thinking of giving his wife everything she wanted in the divorce settlement and

My funny Valentine

having his dog put out of its misery. 'Gosh *why*?' I said on both counts. 'A manic's got to do what a manic's got to do,' he said mournfully. After that the evening started brightening.

I never thought I'd say this, but it *is* 1987 and I'm getting to be an aware person. I've decided you can keep sex, I'm in the market for casual laughter and I'm going to giggle around. You're wonderfully *relaxed* chuckling over dinner, you don't feel rejected if the man doesn't phone after bouts of uninhibited guffaws and you *don't* have to use a condom. In our lifetime no one's going to suggest 'safer laughter'. Send in the clowns.

A thing of beauty is a joy for a fortnight

As I'm writing this someone on Capital Radio is reading out a card from John in Ealing who wants to wish 'Happy Anniversary' to his darling wife Penny whom he met in Mallorca 11 years ago. You don't suppose it was a business trip, do you? It's just that I don't seem to know anyone who has had a holiday romance. 'People say romance when they mean sex,' said my neighbour Ulrik. She's Swedish and she knows about such things. I decided to ask around.

Erich said it was pretty easy to confuse sex and romance but as he was bisexual he was confused about most things these days. Jo said she was doing the ironing and Jennie said she was trying to sleep. Elaine said it was great to be with a man for a few days and then what? Pattie said, 'Don't ask me about holiday romances. I'm having enough trouble in Baker Street with Whatsisname.' Johnnie said that sex and romance on holiday could be disturbing, particularly if you were not with your wife. Selwyn said that no one was meant to have any emotions any more wherever they might be.

Leni said the Italians used to be terrific as far as she remembered. Paul said he liked to be alone even on holiday because all relationships were a massive compromise. Annette said she'd never have met Mel on holiday. In fact, she'd never met *anyone* on holiday.

Ann said, 'Surely you've got to be under 24 to have a holiday romance?' and H said, 'You're not still writing that drivel.' However, he did admit to more than a passing fancy for a girl at Butlins when he was

A thing of beauty is a joy for a fortnight

17. 'Course it was doomed from the start. She lived in Kilburn and that's a long way from Hayes.' Now it could be that my nearest and dearest are not representative of the average girl who heads for a foreign beach with hope in her heart and Moisture Tanning Creme Ultra Strength Sun Protection 8 tucked into her beachbag. Not that *you* are average, of course. None of us is.

Well. I'm your average paranoid who doubts her chance of even finding a *book* that interests her on holiday, let alone a man. These days I take them both with me.

But even then there are no guarantees. I mean I have spent more time on Greek beaches analysing my relationships than anyone I know.

So, if you're lying wistfully on the sand while your girlfriend with the thighs is getting out of her depth with Costas the boatman, you shouldn't necessarily envy the ladies who lured their loved ones to Lindos. It's rarely as good as it looks. The heat and the brilliant sunshine often exacerbate and illuminate all the petty tensions and flaws.

Now is the time when the man will suddenly notice that the woman he has adored for nine months has three non-removable corns, shorter legs than he fondly imagined and not nearly such good tits as that topless French person. The woman is suddenly aware of achingly sexy men around and she can't help feeling that they'd reach the parts of her that her man cannot reach. Because let's face it, an entirely different set of rules applies when you're on a beach.

You *feel* different for a start. Relaxed, full of energy and with an increasing sense of your physical potential. By the time you've jettisoned all your clothes and the Beauty Editor's advice and are massaging 'Savage Tan' into your body, you start to feel positively gift-wrapped inside your own skin.

Normally you need to be *told* that you're looking good. Now you *know*. It's just that you wouldn't mind sharing the terrific new you. It could well be 'anything goes' time. The local men look marvellous, don't they? It's their patch, their beat. They're brown, bold and confident. And genuinely interested in girls, girls, girls. They notice, they flirt, they smile, they invite, they proposition and they don't take 'Go' for an answer.

A thing of beauty is a joy for a fortnight

It's all very seductive to women used to the shrugging indifference of the average Englishman. God *knows* how these men are not suffering from sexual exhaustion by mid-July. But no. They regard each plane and boatload of women that arrive as another opening of another show. And like real troupers, they're always terrific on the night. Course for you they have the added attraction of not having sun-block on their noses, burnt shoulders and Marks & Spencer's striped casual shirts. They look how a man is supposed to look on a beach.

Should you have a romance with one of them? Well, as I said, I never have. I love *looking* at them but I've never had the raw nerve to try one for size. Maybe I think that if I have a fling I'll get flung. I couldn't be romantic for a few days and then forget it ever happened. If I grew to like the native of some far-flung island I'd get back home and wonder why a person who could barely speak English wasn't writing to me. Or else I'd drip listlessly through late August in London moaning to everyone about real life being on Hydra, Sardinia or wherever. And there is the one-night stand possibility that I couldn't take. Rejection would ruin my holiday. I can only take so much lying down. No, the local men are only truly recommended to women who are deliciously uninhibited and oozing self-esteem. They're not for the uncertain or the desperate.

What about the initially-out-of-place Englishmen? Well, they do look better as the holiday wears on. Some of them turn quite presentable shades of brown and once their tongues have stopped hanging out over the Scandinavian blondes they start noticing *you*. Come to think of it, you don't need to get as far as the beach to meet these men.

It's best to meet them in what my friend Annette calls 'the moving transport situation'. On trains, boats and planes. They can be playful at English airports and remarkably good company on the flight to your holiday destination.

With only a couple of hours to score at least an emotional victory, they'll often talk with a charm and intensity that is alien to them the rest of the year. Perhaps you can arrange to go to the beach together. They'll be secretly relieved they don't have to play macho with a topless Teutonic tourist and you may have someone to have dinner with on the first night. No, of course they're not as fascinating as the other men, but

A thing of beauty is a joy for a fortnight

long-term they might prove more reliable – relatively speaking. They're initially vulnerable, which is always an attractive quality in a man. And very few women will be competing for their favours in the early days of the holiday. They might be grateful to have you around. Who knows? You might even arrange to meet for dinner in Covent Garden when the days of wine and poses are over. After the initial cries of, 'I didn't recognise you with your clothes on', you could perhaps form a superficial friendship which may well ripen into something shallower. It's worth a try.

Oh, I guess anything is worth a try when you're in a delicious holiday mood. I've certainly been romantic on holiday with the man I went with and there's nothing to beat it at the time. Inevitably I've suffered from a romantic hangover when I've got back to the solitude of my flat because I am an intimacy junkie. But I do it again every time at the drop of a ticket.

Maybe I'm trying to impress on you that the worst or perhaps the best thing about a holiday romance is that usually it only lasts two weeks. 'A Thing of Beauty is a Joy for a Fortnight' as someone pointed out. Now if *you* think that a thing of duty is a boy for a fortnight I just wanted to mention that the best thing about your holiday romance *could* be that someone somewhere knows you have a brown bottom. If that's enough for you – then go for it. I envy you your cheek.

For those of you who can't face the limited time scale of the holiday love-affair, it might console you to know that according to the National Marriage Guidance Council you stand a better chance of forging a long-term relationship in your local launderette.

Well, it's nice to know, isn't it? When you come home with that pile of clothes covered in oil and sand you do have *something* to look forward to.

Marvellous interesting men

Marvellous interesting men
do it time and time again
though charismatic, intellectual,
they pick a mate who's ineffectual.

She's quite nice looking, rather passive,
her ego's small 'cos his is massive.
She's live-in-love or one-day wife,
he's the sole purpose of her life.

Life's a cherry bowl for him,
she caters to his every whim.
She likes benign dictatorship
and it's 'a good relationship'.

He's fond of her in his own fashion,
his work is normally his passion.
There rarely is an ugly sequel,
his aim is not to find an equal.

His stimulation comes from men,
he comes home to relax again.
He understands his selfish needs,
tends not to bite the hand that feeds.

Course on the side he 'likes a bit',
but he's not leaving home for it.
It's not that sexual highs don't count,
but his home comfort's paramount.

Marvellous interesting men

So if you're challenging and bright
you'd better re-think Mr Right.
And if you want to be a hit
you have to find an opposite.

It works for men which is surprising,
p'raps they don't mind compromising.
The very thought just makes me wince
(my mother promised me a prince).

At least a person my own size
I couldn't bear to compromise.
But women who've a mind to speak
so often run with men who're weak.

Meanwhile marvellous men, you see,
they're not for girls like you and me.
But if you're pretty and you're dumb
then sure as hell your prince will come.

Ex lovers

When wells of passion have run dry,
and love's pronounced a failure,
he should have the decency to die
or leave for South Australia.

Try a little cheerfulness when you feel like thumping him

*I*t was Fiona who suggested this years ago. We were dealing with difficult men, our selfish but it seemed exciting lovers of the time. Fiona was a passionate, funny girl who thought fast on her feet and would do *anything* to make a relationship work. I would do almost anything. And as we discussed *everything* between us we tended to cover most of the possibilities of strategic play with men.

We were sensitive and intelligent people, you understand. We may have had a terrific sense of humour about many aspects of life, but relationships were things we took seriously. Men were not to be taken lightly.

As our consciousness was raised so our tolerance levels were lowered. But you couldn't accuse us of being unaware. Every *nuance* of change in the emotional atmospherics was detected. We analysed every word and every move. And we made damn sure the men *knew* we'd noticed. We instigated discussions about right and wrong behaviour and said, 'That's no way to treat a lady' if the bloke was twenty minutes late, forgot to post a birthday card, fell asleep watching television or wanted to cancel an evening for *whatever reason.*

I was very good at making speeches which started, 'On balance I prefer to be well treated . . .' And I would add the current injustice up with which I no longer intended to put. If that succinct and cute beginning ever did have any effect I blew it by repeating it constantly. We were trying to grow men up. We had decided that we were enor-

Try a little cheerfulness when you feel like thumping him

mously mature, and we thought men should be our wise and caring equals. So we worked at our relationships. Workaholics I suppose you'd have called us. Bloody draining it was too. I mean we were practically *exhausted* with all our commenting, constructive criticism and communicating.

Then Fiona mentioned this amazing and revolutionary new concept for dealing with life in general and men in particular.

'I've tried everything, so now I'm being cheerful,' she said.

'What do you mean?' I said. 'Cheerful' had a kind of stoic, carry on in the face of overwhelming odds, *indifference* that I didn't associate with Fiona.

'I mean *cheerful*,' she said, 'It's a kind of understanding. You don't have to do anything. But you smile a lot and stop talking about the way he should and shouldn't behave. You stop making barbed comments and asking all those questions. Oh and you cut the wry remarks.'

'Gosh,' I said. I mean they were our speciality. Still, Fiona usually knew what she was talking about. She'd done a lot of exploratory work in this field. 'How's it working?' I asked.

'Brilliantly,' she giggled. 'He's been so nice lately. All sort of relaxed and rather affectionate again. You must try it.'

I mulled over the idea. I could see that it might work. Besides which I liked the general idea of cheerfulness. If I thought about the people I loved seeing best they were *cheerful*. Hadn't Marta once described cheerfulness as grace? Hmmmm. It might be interesting not to comment. It would be a personal challenge to smile serenely and appear not to react.

Were our lovers really that tricky? Er yes. Or were they just behaving like men? Er yes. Were we very emotionally demanding? Um yes. Did we expect constant attention because we were sleeping with them? Yes. Did we have any notion of acceptance distance, the fact that our lovers may require more emotional and territorial space than we did? Er no. Did they constantly criticise us and our behaviour? Well no. Were there any wonderful moments? Of course. Were many of our demands due to the fact that we were insecure and wanted constant reassurance? Well now you come to mention it. If we had such a passion for fairness, how

Try a little cheerfulness when you feel like thumping him

fair were we being to the men? Okay, sometimes we were over the top. Could it be that there was right and wrong on both sides and we ought at least to consider the male point of view? I suppose so. Isn't it about time we stopped trying to grow men up? Sure is. I mean wouldn't it be easier on our own heads if we stopped taking them so damned seriously? Where's the fun in all this? You may well ask.

Cheerful has been my philosophy ever since. Look, sometimes I heave myself groaning up the steps marked 'Worried', 'Uncertain', 'Wobbly', 'Depressed' until I reach the one marked 'Cheerful'. And sometimes I don't make it. But these days at least I try. And I try not to step on too many people if I haven't made it. I am not particularly repressed. I don't grin and bear it. I grin and make other arrangements when men get truly tacky. A difficult man trying to provoke a reaction now gets cheerfully ignored. I am provoked much less than I used to be. And I've found men who would be defensive/aggressive fumbling to apologise because I smile and withhold comment.

'Sorry I'm late Marce. I would have phoned but I was held up in traffic.'

'No, doesn't matter,' I say.

'No. But it *does* matter. I said I'd be here at seven thirty and it's gone half past eight.'

'That's fine. Have a drink.'

'No. I'm sorry. I want you to know I'm sorry.'

'That's okay,' I smile.

'It's *so* nice to see you.'

I mean you can go on to have a marvellous evening if you strike the right relaxed and cheerful note in the beginning. Many men, it seems, understand crime and punishment. They're like small boys who expect to be smacked if they misbehave. Well, if you have fantasies about playing mummy to a grown-up male, smack away. Me? I'd rather play cheerful lover.

Once I took cheerful to what I think is the absolute limit. But frankly I didn't have any other ammunition that would have been as effective. Curiously enough it protected me as well as affecting the man I loved. He'd said 'I'm having dinner with some friends. I'll be home later.'

Try a little cheerfulness when you feel like thumping him

'Okay. I'll see you later,' I said. He had an obsession for precise arrival times. I knew he'd be home on the dot of later.

Later got later. And later. And suddenly I had to go to bed because it was getting early. I don't know if dawn and my heart were breaking at exactly the same moment. But I did sit up alone in my double bed wondering about love and if he'd fallen into it. And I thought of crying. Maybe I did. A couple of those soft warm tears that spill when you're very fond of somebody.

While I was sitting there wondering which posture to strike – crumpled/sobbing, ice cold/outraged, furious/passionate – because I felt all of these things, I suddenly remembered cheerful. Inappropriate you think? Well it was the element of surprise that I thought would work. He wouldn't be expecting *cheerful*. I mean you wouldn't, would you? By the time he turned the key in the lock just before eight o'clock I had talked myself into being cheerful.

'Oh darling. You're awake. I was so drunk last night I stayed at John's. I slept so badly. I *missed* you.' He looked anxious.

'Morning,' I said and stretched my arms in what I hoped looked like sleepy pleasure. 'Tea or coffee?'

'I did miss you,' he said. 'God I was drunk. I wanted to come home and sleep with you.'

'Would have been *lovely*,' I smiled. 'Tea or coffee?' He scratched his brow and started to pull nervously at his tie. 'I didn't come *home*,' he insisted. 'It was too late to phone. And you know, I missed you.'

He sat down rather suddenly at the end of the bed looking as forlorn as I'd felt an hour earlier. 'I promise you I had too much to drink,' he said.

Listen, maybe he did, maybe he didn't. Who knows? At that stage if he'd dallied with Bo Derek or drunk two bottles of whisky what could I do to alter history? I wasn't about to end a two-year relationship on the weakness of maybe a one-night stand.

But I wanted to make me feel good and him feel bad. A row would have been too easy. Cheerful left him bewildered and disorientated. He spent days after that trying to be wonderful which I found similarly unnerving. You know, he kept stroking me and staring at me puzzled

Try a little cheerfulness when you feel like thumping him

and saying 'I do love you.'

I knew that cheerful had triumphed when he enthusiastically agreed to watch a documentary on Edvard Munch, my favourite tortured painter. I mean Liverpool were playing Arsenal on the other channel. He only glanced at his watch once at what would have been half time . . .

I don't know who said, 'I never promised you a rose garden.' But I do wish that inside and outside of relationships, people, for their own sakes, would grasp the fact that things weren't *meant* to be easy all the time. Sometimes life and people are a pleasure. At other times there is pain and stress. It's what living in the eighties and any other time is all about.

Contrary to what you may think, there are no such things as 'charmed lives'. My mother used to talk about people having 'everything' and I believed her. I guess what's really important is your perception of what's good rather than agonising over what's bad. Or as Jo once put it, 'Isn't it *amazing* how we tend to concentrate on the 10 per cent that *isn't* working for us?'

So I'm putting forward cheerful as a self-protection, as a way of attracting other people towards you, as a social obligation, as an alternative to depression, as a new perception. Do you remember, 'Two men looked through prison bars. One saw mud the other stars'?

Of course the dangers of cheerful are that you develop a full-time delicious sense of humour which is a very powerful weapon indeed. Are you ready for that?

Your body: what a woman really wants

A man asked me to write this. 'You're just the person,' he said. 'What *really* turns you on about a man's body?' 'Er. I don't know,' he said. 'I mean, if you talk to women you find there are parts of men that really *excite* them. Hard chests, tight arses. Women adore tight arses. Good biceps, muscular thighs.' 'Ooh, I like all that,' I said. 'But those parts only turn you on if you are attracted by the man anyway.'

'Well,' he said, 'just say what would turn you on about a man you didn't know. Describe all the bits you'd find special. Oh, and mention his penis. Men are very hung up about the size of their penis.' 'I thought they were all six inches extended,' I mumbled. 'Do men really worry about them?' 'God yes,' he said. '*Terribly* important. I mean men's bodies are very important to a lot of women.' 'I suppose they would be,' I said. 'You mean you'd like me to write about the male equivalent of "tits and arse"?' 'That's exactly right,' he said. 'Say what *really turns you on*. Keep it very *physical*. Can you do it?'

'Yes,' I lied. And I've been puzzling about the different way that men and women react to each other ever since. Women don't hang around bookstalls furtively flicking through the pages of *Playgirl*. No female I ever knew wanted a date with a man because he was 'well stacked'. And the last time I heard a woman mention 'an enormous penis' it was an embarrassed complaint. For better or worse we are not that interested in anonymous male bodies. We do not stand in nudging groups whistling and cat-calling because a great-looking male body strolls by. God I wish

Your body: what a woman really wants

it were that easy to be turned on. I would be racing on to building sites and dragging shirtless, sinewy men into the car. 'You're irresistible,' I would yell. 'Those muscled arms. Those gorgeous shoulders, You can't parade around like that and not expect to be jumped on.' Well they *do* parade around like this and in my admittedly limited experience the average well-constructed construction worker does *not* expect to be jumped on just because he goes topless. Most women are not as easily aroused as men. Their sexual consciousness, like their vaginas, has to be penetrated. Even women who sleep with lots of men often do so out of a desire for intimacy rather than because they were hopelessly 'turned on'. Or else they're thinking, 'Maybe this time . . .' Sex is so readily available to most of us that what we wait for is the all-elusive *chemistry*. The turn-on. Mostly it's about timing. And contact.

Once I was sitting in a restaurant next to a man I'd been out with a few times. It was a warm evening. I was wearing a barely nothing T-shirt and he had his shirt sleeves rolled up. At one point our arms touched and I felt the bright shock of male hair brushing along my forearm. I stared at his profile and then at his tanned arm where the dark hairs curled deliciously over his watchstrap. That was the beginning of a very big turn-on. I love male arms. It must be that line 'to have and to hold' from the marriage ceremony. The only thrilling line I always think.

I have to admit I don't even want to think about a connection with a man who is fat. The plumpness I often find so attractive on a woman I dislike on a man. Fatty deposits on the female are frequently part of her sexuality but I've never understood why a man should get fat. I'm not biased or anything, it's just that I sleep with men. Mind you, too slim is not appealing. That can look boyish and I don't go for boys. But there is a kind of filled-out lean, a ripeness that makes me want to touch, grab and pinch. It probably belongs to a six-footer who thinks he ought to lose about seven pounds. You know, I probably like a male version of myself. A man with medium-broad shoulders, slightly tanned skin, slim ankles and wrists and a very male chest. A very male chest has very male, soft thick hair and obvious pectoral muscles. It is a sight – when I realise there is a soft heart beating inside the chest – that weakens me with pleasure.

Your body: what a woman really wants

A chest is definitely one of my favourite parts, but such is the stuff that love is made of that I was once besotted by a wild American who had no hair on his chest. Hair might have ruined everything. He did have skin like butter and the only arse I've ever consciously noticed. He also had a two-inch spider tattooed on his right buttock. Totally cured me of my phobia. Of spiders, I mean. He had a small, firm, wriggly arse and one of his philosophies was, 'If you've got it, flaunt it.' He flaunted me all the way into bed and I didn't get up for two years. Many women do mention arses but I think it's just the female version of macho chat – fashionable, tough sexual patter. Anyway these days I like buttocks firm and inconspicuous.

I like hair – curly hair and thick hair and soft hair and straight hair and fine hair and, currently, I like blondish-brown hair that flops over one eye so that elegant fingers have to be run through it to put it back into place. It's endearing to watch a man who considers himself controlling unable to control his own hair. The same man has surprisingly long lashes. When we're arguing politics and the green eyes narrow as a serious point is made, I look at the frivolous lashes and think, 'But I know who's *really* in there.' The same lashes brush my cheek. The same lashes look wonderful when he is asleep. Silky, girly, feathery fastenings that look even better on this man.

Long strong legs are very aesthetically pleasing. They should be straight with *lightly* developed thighs. All in all, muscle-bound men are out. Men may well find Miss World a turn-on but no woman I know would be seen dead with Mr. Universe. Over-developed men look so ridiculous in clothes, and who wants a man whose obvious priority in life is *his* body?

I forgive a great deal of a man with beautiful, capable hands. I always suspect that he has character and intelligence. It's nice to watch firm male hands grip a steering wheel, stroke a whisky glass and carry a case. And as for hands that do dishes – that could be the ultimate turn-on. Last Monday I had a positively thrilling half-hour watching a man at Christie's do deals on the phone, make rapid notes, stretch long fingers across catalogues and play with his pen while he talked. Nice face, nice suit, nice manner. The hands were mesmerising. They actually led me to

Your body: what a woman really wants

wonder what sort of forearms and upper arms and shoulders they led up to, and then where the chest might lead down to. I wonder what sort of women turn him on ...?

This sort of woman did not wonder, fantasise or even think about his penis. I can say from experience, and I also have it on strict medical authority from Dr Lenard Jacobsen (a noted American urologist) that, as I said, extended they're pretty much the same. It's truly difficult for the average woman to understand why men attach so much importance to the size of a penis in its unaroused state. Heaven knows what men say or think in the men's shower room. It's the 'growth' and how it fits that is exciting to the female. I've never stared at one that was small and thought, 'This is not worth the effort.' Two of my absolutely favourite lovers, men to whom I was positively sexually addicted, did not sport large power bulges. Thinking about it now, they must have extended to fill me. And I do seem to remember that a penis will vary in size at different times during the sexual act. One can only conclude that a woman who whips out a magnifying glass to disdainfully inspect a small penis does not know very much about men. Men who discuss sizes and feel like terrific jocks because they have 'a big one' cannot understand very much about women. I can only tell you that being turned on and in love counts more than size. There are men who disappoint and men who thrill and men who *hold* you in such a confident and caring way that the two of you feel that you were made to fit together. Men who feel wonderful are rare. Probably men feel the same way about women. A penis has never turned me on. One or two men to whom they are attached have pleasured me almost unbearably.

Sorry about bodies. I mean, I have been tremendously fond of them, absolutely wild about them. But I was in love. And how on earth do you explain that to men who want to know just about being turned on? It's rarely as simple as that. I probably wouldn't have said any of these things to a woman. But a man asked me to write this.

Dinner date

I have just come home from dinner
with the great love of my life.
He looked greyer. I am thinner,
he's still bored with his ex-wife.
He came sharp at seven-thirty
and I poured the usual drinks.
I was pleasant but unflirty
Do I care now what he thinks ...?

He showed mild enthusiasm
as we chatted inter-course
but I felt no sexual spasm
for my former *tour-de-force*.
We discussed our current living,
yes his eyes and shirt still matched ...
he's attractive, I'm forgiving
and I stared at him, detached.

I began to wonder whether
I had dreamed the things we'd said.
Were we truly so 'together'?
I'd forgotten us in bed.
Had this stranger really mattered?
Were his eyes always that cold?
All my fantasies were shattered
I decided he looked old ...

Dinner date

Had I hoped for some improvement
in the man I'd loved and prized?
Did the lack of my heart movement
leave me wretchedly surprised?
All those memories I'd savoured,
all those bitter tears I'd shed,
over claret love had wavered
and by cognac love was dead.

No, he hadn't really altered
I'd just seen him through rose-tints
Can I blame him that we faltered
and so much has happened since ...?
P'raps I'm glad I went for dinner,
some things start when others end
He did say he liked me thinner ...
P'raps I'll be his slender friend.

Ex-rated lovers

*W*hen people say accusingly,
'Why do you see your ex-lovers?' they infer that they are men of less
value than a trashy novel. And, God knows, you know the plot so why
do you keep them around? Well, I've rarely wasted my time on cheap
paperbacks. I'm mad about good books.

I may not curl up with them with the same wonderment or sense of
abandon that I felt on that first reading. But I do love to re-read them. I
love to discover passages I'd missed, to discover certain truths which had
escaped me. Maybe I feel sadness because I have a tendency to masochistic sentimentality and I want a fresh explanation of a bad chapter. Oh but
then there are the irresistibly funny bits and I can laugh as never before.
Throw away my ex-lovers? Are you crazy? They are part of me. Part of
my emotional and social furniture. Of course I love them. Differently. I
may not sleep with them. Or if I do it is no longer with the same fraught
intensity. Well – perhaps that too has happened.

Having said all that, it's not good my pretending that some of these
friendships I now hold dear were easily forged in the beginning. I mean
in the beginning after the end. You see it's very hard to recognise 'the
end'. Perhaps it is easy for some people, but personally speaking I
experience great problems owing to my superbly developed denial
process. I'm very good at telling myself and anyone else who'll listen
that 'we're just going through a bad patch'.

And even when it has been me yelling 'I never want to see you again as
long as I live' I've always assumed that tomorrow my lover and I would
be tenderly reunited. Some men have taken those words very personally
and I've had the devil of a job explaining what I meant.

I suppose that when two people are lovers – by this I mean that they
care for each other as well as sleep together – there is often the expectation on one or both sides that the affair may lead Somewhere. The one
with the expectation is usually the woman. She frequently isn't clear in

Ex-rated lovers

her own mind exactly what she wants, but what she *doesn't* want is for her lover to call a halt or meet another woman before she's ready. I have rarely been prepared to end an affair and it's just as well I've had some clear-headed lovers. I've found that men are invariably more decisive in these matters. I would linger on like someone at a summer holiday place when the cold days of the end of the season have arrived. Sometimes, despite dull agony, it's been a relief to get back home to myself again. I'm not saying that I haven't felt wretched. Just that the lack of tension when an affair is *over* is easier than the ending of the affair.

It does take time. Sometimes months or even years to complete the required stages of anger and bitterness, grief and finally acceptance. The point where you dream up awful revenge, wish he'd emigrate or pray that he'll break both legs is not the time to say, 'I can't *believe* we're not friends after all that.'

What is for sure is that only when you *accept* the fact that the affair as you knew it is over are you free to be friendly. Before that it's possible to delude yourself that a meeting with your ex-lover might lead to a magical resurrection of love and romance. You may even be led into believing that spending the night with him will somehow catapult you back into the affair. This comes under the heading of a Desperate Act although it's all too easy to deceive yourself he still cares in the same way because sex does seem mysteriously like loving.

Don't ask me if I've done it. Of course I've done it. The very best people make fools of themselves. Mind you, there are two schools of thought here. Mine and every psychiatrist I've spoken to. Sex between ex-lovers is destined to remain a tricky area. Terrible misunderstandings can arise. Women may find it hard to believe they're no longer loved but men find it impossible to grasp the fact that you no longer wish to sleep with them. It has been very clearly demonstrated to me that while I'm basking in what I think is pure affection, an ex-lover is puzzled and seemingly hurt by the fact I no longer wish to go to bed with him.

'But we love each other,' he'll moan with the touching vulnerability of a man whose parking meter has another hour to run and whose lady-love of four years is waiting at home with a cooked meal. But male-like I too have made this mistake. I once had a wonderful day with an ex-lover

Ex-rated lovers

in New York. He was a man I desired but was no longer certain that I loved. We leaped out into Manhattan's streets at ten in the morning and combed the Lower East Side and lunched in Greenwich Village and shopped in Saks and Macy's and saw a film and had dinner and staggered back to his hotel full of parcels and togetherness.

'Such a perfect day,' I thought as I started to undress. He was furious. 'How *dare* you think you can just spend the night with me?' he growled.

Whoops! How dare I indeed? That was ultimately what I would call a useful learning experience. I am no longer angry with ex-lovers who think they can spend the night with me.

A great deal of your ability to see ex-lovers depends on your current happiness. Such meetings are best when you're feeling strong and secure and preferably have fallen in love again. I have at times over-estimated my inner peace. Just when I've thought that God's in his heaven and all's right with my world, an ex will arrive looking seriously attractive, successful and thrilled with life. As I pour him a Scotch I'm envious of who he's with, where he's going and the way he manages to look so damned happy without me. When he has departed I survey what I then perceive as my hollow life and wonder how I thought my current affair could ever match up to this love I once knew. I'm assured that men too experience these masochistic moments.

Ex-lovers look even more mouth-wateringly attractive when your life is packed with non-events. One of my friends is now tearfully insisting that she would have married the man who certainly wasn't what she had in mind at the time of the affair. But the bliss of ex-lovers is normally the lack of expectation on both sides. During the affair the two people concerned seem to put each other through a series of subtle tests. It can be very serious stuff because the future and the way it may be determined hangs in the balance. Ex-lovers no longer test each other. Well, maybe just a bit. To see if they're still loved. But it's a harmless and rather endearing game.

Of course this marvellous lack of tension can lead to some rather confusing emotions. You may well spend time wondering why, if you can now get along so well, you didn't manage to harness this warm,

Ex-rated lovers

tactile compatibility in the first place. People around you are building lives and families on about 20 per cent of what you two seem to have had going for you. The answer is that it's only because you are now free of demands and expectation that you have the luxury of behaving tenderly each time you meet.

I remember sitting in the cocktail bar of a hotel having a drink with the man with whom I'd lived. He was so warm as he revealed some touching personal and financial truths. I stared at the face of the man I'd loved so painfully and said, 'You're so honest and exposed these days. Why weren't you like this when we were together?' He looked puzzled, then said, 'We were too close. This takes time. I suppose you're my best friend.' He's right. It does take time. I would have been awful to have missed the Second Act. How does the practice of seeing your ex-lovers affect the current person in your life? The rule must be that you will not jeopardise the current relationship because you insist on seeing your ex-lover. Either introduce them and hope for the best or see your ex without hurting or threatening the current man. God knows, I've practically always come unstuck here. I'm terrific at the theory. The current man has rarely shown the same degree of unbridled enthusiasm that I've felt for an ex-lover. And at worst the current man has thought the ex might be 'useful'. Comments have ranged from 'What did you see in him?' to 'I know you still find him attractive', to 'I've heard he's lousy in bed', to 'He's rather short, isn't he?'

And I've rarely been treated to the sight of, let alone an evening, with my ex-lover's new woman. Will I be too critical? Will I suspect he and his new love don't have what *we* had? Will I suspect he's *truly* in love this time? Would he just as soon she didn't know that he'd been involved with someone like me? Who the hell knows? I've never figured it out. I've just accepted the fact that my ex-lovers tend to keep their lives compartmentalised and albeit grudgingly, I respect it. Yes I am aware that some happy foursomes are composed of two ex-lovers and their new lovers. But it does smack of something slightly incestuous and I've often wondered if all four people were as relaxed as they appeared. There's always that private historical territory between two ex-lovers that's sealed from the rest of the world. And that can be unsettling to the

Ex-rated lovers

most recent person to enter a life.

Of course, current lovers in people's lives tend to be wary of ex-lovers. They wonder what went wrong, how important the two people were to each other and if there is ever a possibility of them 'getting back together' again either for a night or for life. But ultimately, they have very little reason to be wary. Most of what's going to happen has already happened. Ex-lovers who are great friends are two people who have forgiven each other the disappointments and remembered the pleasures. Only in exceptional circumstances do they become lovers again; mostly I agree with my ex-lovers that it's easier to meet in a one-to-one situation or with great friends. But almost always *without* one's current involvement. It's too inhibiting. Mostly it's delicious just to keep in touch, to reassure, be reassured, to help, advise, stroke a familiar arm and ask how you're supposed to run your current man. Ex-lovers are very wise and forthcoming about other men when they're not subjected to them personally.

Ex-lovers have buoyed me up and carried me through crises in my life with a protectiveness they rarely showed when I was with them. An ex-lover is free to express all those marvellous things he may have forgotten to tell you at the time. You may hear that he thinks about you often and sometimes he misses you. This sort of chat makes you feel very good about yourself. It tells you that your initial judgement about a loving man was absolutely correct and it was, after all, worth going through 'all that' to become such good friends.

Can you go back to ex-lovers? Well it's certainly been known. It's curious what can happen in life. One woman I know married an ex-lover thirty years later even though they'd both been married in the interim years. Two other friends who'd raggedly kept in touch through love affairs and a marriage by one of them married 13 years later on the anniversary of the day they met. And didn't you read in the papers about the GI, now 67, who'd come back to Britain to marry the woman he'd had an affair with in the 1940s.

Me? I think I may have fallen in love with an ex-lover of fifteen years ago. Who'd have thought it after all these years?

Throw away my ex-lovers? Never.

Having fun with Mr Wrong

*M*r Right is elusive. Or he's with the Woolwich. Oh you know him. He's that dependable, mildly attractive man who reeks of the sweet scent of security. He has a lifestyle that you understand or aspire to. You appreciate his thinking, his background and the marvellous way your friends and interests so easily intertwine. However successful you may be in your own right, you do get the distinct impression that he'd be prepared to guard you, guide you, keep you, feed you if necessary. Family and friends are delighted.

'Oh he's so *right* for you,' they chorus. You can always turn to him because he's always there. That sturdy, soft, subtly woven fabric that when wrapped around you will protect you from life's chill winds. Husband material.

Many women have a fairly fixed idea about Mr Right. And while they'll happily experiment in the early days of dating and waiting, later on they become what they call 'choosy'. This often means they choose not to entertain the idea of dating men who fall short of their ideals. They tell themselves it's a waste of time to see men who don't fit their socio-economic and intellectual requirements.

Well I've met Mr Right more than once. And what was so surprising was that this eminently suitable man, this person who was everything I thought I had In mind, didn't suit me. Yet Mr Wrong, who was frequently most unsuitable in terms of all the 'standards' I had set has afforded me more pleasure, fun and even longevity than many of the men who seemed right. I was still having fun with various Mr Wrongs

Having fun with Mr Wrong

while two of my girlfriends managed to get engaged, married, have children and get divorced.

You do find that life is suddenly fraught with fascinating possibilities once you stop demanding the maximum and start considering the optimum qualities of the man you meet. What is so positively terrific is that you have so many options once you cease the obsessive search for Mr Right. Your choice is limitless – most men you meet are wrong for you.

The whole thing is a bit like a masked ball anyway. You don't know who you're dancing with. Men disguised as good husband material so often aren't, whereas young leaping lovers and shaky movers in later years turn out to be the most desirable of mates. So unless you seek the peaks of excitement offered by an allround formation dancer, why not give a non-conformist partner a whirl? He may teach you steps you never knew.

When I decided that married I could always get, I stopped bemoaning the fact that the raunchy American I was seeing was an out-of-work musician instead of a stockbroker. Before, if anyone had ever told me that I'd be having a thing of beauty in Battersea with a sounds freak whose equipment room looked like the nerve centre at Cape Canaveral – I'd never have believed them. He rarely read a book and I understood almost nothing about the music he loved. But he took me to rock concerts, taught me to appreciate classical music and when I was frazzled after a day at the office showed me the only way to r-e-l-a-x. He cooked the best breakfast ever and he lingered over meals and sex in a way that enchanted me. He never looked at the time and so it seemed to stand still. Well, he never had to be anywhere. ...

What *he* really had in mind was a graceful young blonde who'd effortlessly produce *cordon bleu* meals and blonde children. But he had me, a graceless redhead with kitchen phobia. Well, I suppose I could have dyed the children's hair – but frankly I had my time cut out getting my own tint right.

With all that we didn't have in common, the chemistry was so good that sometimes we played 'if only'. If only I were in my early twenties, domesticated and understood just a little more about Beethoven. Or any

Having fun with Mr Wrong

oven. I fought Bach with: if only he'd earn some money, was less obsessed with fair haired ladies and was able to communicate with just *one* of my friends.

But we enjoyed such funny, tender moments. Because of him I appreciate baseball, wild flowers and the Albert Bridge. Because of him I learned that you don't have to 'attack' life. Sometimes it can simply flow over you and you can relax and enjoy it. I still wear on my little finger a heart-shaped ring he gave me. We'd scraped souls, accepted different interests and he remains a loving friend. The wrong man who has so many right qualities.

Wrong men, men you don't readily understand, can so often stretch you, make you think laterally. They can add immeasurably to your mental and emotional equipment. They're character building. And if you are the sum total of your experiences, you don't add up to much if you haven't allowed yourself to enjoy many 'experiences'. Yes, it can be a rollercoaster ride, but ... it's exhilarating.

I remember trying to come to grips with Scott, an urgently attractive writer and film producer. It was initially impossible to fathom the workings of his devious and sophisticated mind. He called me Zelda. He also called me cynical and wry. He had the wickedest grin and the softest skin and he taught me to survive in an age of vulgarity. God knows if he ever knew how out of my depth I felt at times. To him the 'element of surprise' was an essential ingredient in a relationship. I learned to expect the unexpected, learned that you don't have to be sure of anyone except yourself. Forget possessive. No one had ever possessed such a man. Such an avid believer in life, liberty and the happiness of pursuit would have withered in an enclosed, monogamous life. He sharpened my mind, my wits and my humour. It would have been hard not to fall in love with him.

The good surprises delighted me. He sent me a Dupont lighter when I didn't smoke, sent telegrams asking for dates and had a 12 foot balloon delivered to my office, with written instructions about its upkeep and further education. He once wrote me a letter telling me never to lose my insecurity. It was he who told me, 'Next time you're in love with someone, tell him. You have to make yourself vulnerable in life.'

Having fun with Mr Wrong

The wrong men do often say and understand the right things. They may not have their own lives worked out in a comprehensible fashion but they do pass on some useful tips – the sort of information that other people neglect to tell you. Reinforcement of the ideas you already have does *not* help your growth.

Some wrong men may be just about fun and company and a little bit of love along the way. The right wrong men are always people you care about. But you do have to *accept* them and what they have to offer and not start making unreasonable demands or comparisons. Sometimes exposure helps eliminate certain subconscious prejudices you may have about people. Equally it may make you reassess certain cherished beliefs you have about others. All rich men are not playboys or workaholics, all accountants are not dull, all men in advertising are not dynamic, most show-business people are not fascinating. Eccentric, creative men are no more liable to give you a hard time than a man who is Something in the City and all very good-looking men are not spoiled or dumb. Frequently it's the nice, 'safe' men who deliver the body punches because your defences are down and your *expecting* 'right' behaviour. When a tentative Mr Right left me alone on a dangerous birthday, it was a Mr Wrong of many years standing who suggested going on safari in Kenya. He didn't want wild sex. He wanted wildlife and African adventures. 'Best holiday I've had in years,' he said on our last night in Nairobi.

'That's because we're wrong for each other,' I explained. I hadn't minded his purple and orange swimming trunks, he hadn't objected to my eyelash curlers and he hadn't accused me of unnatural sexual acts when I'd spent Christmas lunch with a Masai tribesman. He was terrifically sporting about my amoebic dysentery and only a few weeks ago he came to rescue me when my car got stuck in the car wash.

Somewhere in a drawer is a collection of letters and telegrams. They portray the range of emotions of the wrong men I've known. They vary from, 'I'd marry you anytime, anywhere,' to 'I wouldn't touch you with a disinfected barge pole.' Well, some men are more wrong than others. I have a postcard from the wrongest man I loved the most. It shows a view of the gas works near a slag heap in a mining town. The postcard is black and white. The sky behind the gasworks is wretched leaden grey.

Having fun with Mr Wrong

The forlorn writing says, 'I miss you.' It's the perfect postcard. He gave me my first ever dressing gown – 'You can't meet the window cleaner in a green bath towel' – and an insight into the anatomy of a divorce. He suffered, she agonised and I checked in to a psychiatrist.

What's good about Mr Wrong is that you *can* indulge in the same heartbreak, sleepless nights and masochism as you can with the right man. I promise you it feels just like the real thing. A girl with the wrong man need never feel deprived. I lived for him, with him and in spite of him. He strained my tolerance to the limit, the gentlest, funniest most unreasonable man I've ever known. We agreed that we adored each other, but that was the only point of real agreement. He taught me to say 'No' to people who demanded too much of my time, but the man who said, 'A friend in need is a pain in the arse,' would put his friends before anyone else. He would have liked me fatter, I wanted him to lose weight. I craved peace and intimacy at the cottage in the country. His idea of rural calm was 12 people for Sunday lunch. He slept when we went to the theatre, but always had a strong point of view about the merits of the play. His best and most original ideas would come to him at four in the morning when he'd prod my comatose body and say, 'Are you asleep?' I *never* knew when to expect him home. 'We're seeing a film,' could mean two cheap seats at the ABC Queensway or a Gala Première. He normally forgot to say. I was one of the few souls who pulsated to the opening night of *Saturday Night Fever* in a grey pleated skirt and sweater. The only woman at the Royal Première of *Evita* outshone by the usherettes. 'You look wonderful to me,' he whispered as he helped me into my sock-it-to-'em beige Aquascutum mac and helped Joan Collins into her drab full-length white mink. She told me consolingly that most men were impossible. He was possibly the most impossible. My all time favourite man. He was perhaps a man for all seasons. It's just that his seasons didn't coincide with mine. Or maybe it was that the football season lasted ten months at a time when I didn't appreciate the subtleties of the game. Just when I became a *Match of the Day* fanatic, he told me the game had lost its charm. He taught me that if I could survive life and love with him, I could survive anybody – provided they loved me and made me laugh.

Having fun with Mr Wrong

Don't ask me what's the point in all this. Romance, fun, experience, learning, laughing and loving. That's the point. Mr Wrong is the perfect pleasure – exquisite, unfinished. I couldn't have imagined life without him. Hedda Gabler said she married because she danced till she was tired. I intend to dance till I'm *exhausted*. Save me the waltz Mr Wrong.

Man's best friend

A wicked little cartoon book was published a few months ago. It is called *Man's Best Friend* and its originators are two men called Gray Jolliffe and Peter Mayle. Their names seem to fuse in the mind as Jolly Male and so, if you're like me, you feel quite benign about the book even before you've flicked through the pages. Jolliffe, who did the drawings, said he thought that men might identify with the hero. Indeed they did. And thousands of women recognised him too, although they seemed less amused to read about his life and hard times.

Despite initial objections from some booksellers who declined to stock 'that sort of thing' the little book climbed rapidly into the bestseller lists. It's not your average funny book. But much of its success is due to the fact that Jolliffe and Mayle – unwittingly perhaps – have simply and humorously hit upon a great psychological truth. They've come out and said what most men know and few women wish to acknowledge. Man's Best Friend is his penis. Gosh. All I can say is it's a relief that someone has finally put this invaluable piece of information in print. I would add that it should be required reading for all women who like to go out – and stay in – with men. It will serve to remind you that sooner or later if you're seeing a Man, you will be exposing yourself to *two* people. If you want a 'loving relationship' – remember them? – you have to be liked by the Man as well as the Best Friend. This odd couple frequently have differing tastes, needs, enthusiasms and boredom thresholds. It has been known for them not to agree on the choice of sexual partner. Or if you've ever felt that you were seeing a Man with a split personality you were probably right.

Jolliffe and Mayle, who stand to lose everything but royalties, have

Man's best friend

been glaringly honest and pretty uncharitable about Man's Best Friend. The penis, Wicked Willie, is depicted as a hero in the Andy Capp mould. Frankly he's not at all the kind of person with whom you'd wish to associate. He's 'lazy ... selfish ... unreliable ... demanding ... behaves badly ... and is fond of low company ...' Whether or not you'd apply the term 'best friend' to such a person is debatable. But what this book does convey better than any textbook I've ever read is the peculiarly schizoid behaviour of the male.

The Best Friend, the alter ego, the penis, wants what he wants when he wants it. He sends messages to the Man, who is then forced to take certain action to gratify his Best Friend. This is why a whole lot of men suddenly find themselves being ridiculously charming and lying through their teeth to a woman they don't actually *like* simply to get her into bed.

Once the Best Friend has had his way, he flops happily down to rest leaving the Man and the Woman alone with their lack of thoughts. The Man, who probably didn't want to go to bed with the Woman in the first place, is then left to solve the eternal male problem, How Do I Get Out Of Here? Men are often amazed to find themselves in this situation. They are irritable and bad-tempered at being left to extricate themselves. 'Huh! Some Best Friend,' they think. Course, we women haven't a clue what is going on. 'Has the world gone *mad*?' we think, when we watch the Man who was practically melting at our feet a few hours before turn into a cold, alien creature who can't wait to get into his trousers and out through the front door. Thinking of a Man as two people at this point – or better still the night before – may not help you feel any better. But at least it might *explain* what's going on. That way you won't have to ring *your* best friend and say, 'What the hell did I do? I mean, I thought we were getting on well and he liked me and the next thing I knew he'd gone and he hasn't even asked to see me again.' Or words to that effect. The sorrowful truth is you were taken in by penis-speak. God knows it can be pretty convincing chat. And most of us are dying to be convinced that someone likes us and finds us attractive. It's partly naïveté and partly a trick of nature to perpetuate the species. But more than that it seems to be a sort of cock-eyed optimism which leads women into bed with men

Man's best friend

who've demonstrated little else other than a need for sex. A you-never-know-this-may-lead-to-something attitude. Worst of all, despite Man's Best Friend's well-documented *lack* of selectivity, women are still *flattered* when a Man expresses a wish to sleep with them.

Listen, of *course* you can get a Man via his Best Friend. But only if you sense the Man is interested in you as well. Powerful chemistry is rare. It is not to be confused with a hope against hope that some Man with whom you have no special rapport will fall in love with you – or you with him – just because you responded to his genital thinking. Unless you've stumbled across a Man who is a virgin you are unlikely to become a sudden addiction. But women are not only optimists. They're very good at self-deception. They see what they want to see and hear what they want to hear. It doesn't seem to matter that the Man is not particularly tender, pleasant or understanding. They don't seem to notice that the Man is doing most of the talking, manipulative, can't-wait-to-get-you-into-bed stuff. It all sounds good to a Woman who's yearning for 'a relationship'. He wants to sleep with me, ergo I *please* him.

Sometimes a Man will have penis-speak developed into what is practically an art form. I once shared a flat with an easy-going, rather good-looking Man who every so often would come home from work and say, 'I have to get laid this evening.' He'd get out his battered address book, get on the phone and starting with the 'A's he'd systematically ring every 'passable' Woman who might be available. It was nerve-wracking being another Woman listening to his incredible patter. 'Oh God say you're busy,' I used to pray silently as I heard him go through his routine. But 'Amanda/Antonia/Fiona/Diana/Suzie/Jane/Somebody you looked absolutely *marvellous* the other evening/day/weekend. I *must* see you. Are you free for dinner this evening?' rarely failed. Because they were the days of the cursory phone calls the morning after, he'd ring with a brief, 'Great to see you. I'll be in touch.' And that would be that. He didn't get in touch unless he developed another urge to 'get laid' or he needed an escort. 'Taking Amanda to that damned ball,' he'd say.

Another married Man friend of mine told how a Man feels when faced

Man's best friend

with a Woman he has the urge to sleep with. 'It's incredible how all you can think about is getting the woman into bed,' he said. 'I sit there knowing full well I ought to be getting home because my wife is expecting me and I said I'd see to the bookshelves and walk the dog and pop around to the Wilsons. Yet if I can get the girl to come out to dinner with me I ring home with the most idiotic excuses. I take the girl back to her flat and go to bed with her and honestly at that precise moment nothing is more important than making love to this marvellous, willing, available creature. I tell you when I can feel the sperm rushing up my penis I think I may explode with excitement. But the instant it's all over, *all* I can think about is *Christ* I told Anna I'd see to the bookshelves. I haven't walked that poor dog for *days*. And the Wilsons. God the Wilsons. How can I let *them* down? If I get out of here very fast and beat it down the motorway we could just get there in time for a nightcap . . .'

Men frequently seem astonished that women are prepared to accept so little and put up with so much. 'Your sex are amazing,' a seriously good-looking journalist said to me. 'I mean I behave atrociously, take some girl to bed, don't even bother to call, didn't even bother to buy her dinner. And just when I'm feeling slightly guilty and feel I ought to apologise, the girl rings me and says *she's* sorry about the evening. And can she see me again. What *is* it with you lot?'

Does all this start to make you cynical about men? Well, maybe that's not such a bad thing. It's better than being gullible. Jolliffe and Mayle probably deserve an award for Outstanding Service to Females. They've done us a big favour with the publication of *Man's Best Friend*. Now it's just a question of us sorting out who we're dealing with – but at least we've been warned.

Jolliffe says, 'Being a man *is* like being two people. Women should recognise that and only be prepared to be taken on by the *team*.' Gosh. You'd better buy the book.

Plea to Scott

Scott Fitzgerald please come back
all of us are going to crack.
It's sad as hell you went away
D'you know you died on my birthday?
P'raps that's why I hate it so
men like you should *never* go.

Dearest Scott the world has changed
the whole damn system's re-arranged
Marriage now starts with divorce
(after one's knocked-up of course).
It's then the man will 'leave' his wife
with whom he vowed to spend his life.

Well, yes he left her years before
but honestly who's keeping score?
You live with him, he lives with you
for a year or maybe two.
He never says 'please marry me'
(that's why he's not divorced you see).

My girlfriends now accept the fact
their lives won't have a second act.
Unless they're devious and smart
so weary head rules saddened heart.
Reluctantly against their will
one tender night they miss 'the pill'.

Plea to Scott

Eight weeks on and feeling worse
they tell the man they've missed the curse.
F. Scott Fitz, what you went through
to get 'the girl' to marry *you*.
And pregnancy was marvellous news
'Eighties man has other views.

He staggers slowly, groans out 'F-U-C-K'
(you drank champagne and blessed your luck).
His rage grows to immense proportion
he suggests a swift abortion.
He had his children years before
and definitely does not want more.

Now it's tears and they don't speak
he's catatonic for a week.
Finally, his hand is forced
she'll keep the child, he'll get divorced.
(His wife is not reduced to tears
they've lived apart for seven years.)

Months roll on and she grows bigger
he resents she's lost her figure.
On odd days he doesn't mind
other times he's so unkind.
In the end he's meek and mild
after all it is *his* child.

At the birth he'll hold her hand
no, Scott, marriage isn't planned.
Grudgingly it's 'wait and see'
he's concerned with child-to-be.
Son and heir *must* bear his name
thank heaven for the deed-poll game.

Plea to Scott

They marry when the child is one
aren't the nineteen-eighties fun?
Dearest Scott in Paradise
please come back we need advice.
Frankly I may not survive
hurry while I'm still alive.

Sorry I spoke

Oh, no. I can see your face glazing over. Is it because I've mentioned the word *relationship*? You think it's all been said and done and written about ad nauseam? You'd like to get on with life without all this analysing? Women would too. It's just that things between us have never been resolved. What do you *want*? You never say. We're in the dark on this side of the bed. You seem to be less enthusiastic about us than you used to be. What did we *do*? Doesn't the woman of today appeal to you? I tell you we need you just as much as ever. We're not emotionally independent, you know. Honestly, I thought you'd say, 'Well done. We're proud of you.' But no. You're still rushing into the arms of dependent women who will accept anything as long as they have *you*. Or you're digging your heels in. Or you've retired bewildered. *You're* confused? How d'you think it feels on this side? I was thinking of saving up for a partial lobotomy. No, I realize you don't want to be challenged all the time. Who does? But what about love and life with a soul mate, a person your own size and weight? Too stressful an idea? The thought never occurred to you? Is the idea of being best friends with the woman you sleep with truly out of the question?

Sorry I spoke. Yes, of course the idea is absurd. No, I won't bring it up again. Friends and lovers, two different words. Of course *lover* is the noun from the verb *to love*. Okay, okay. Yes, of course I understand that I am talking about sex. Silly me. Well, do you know what sex means to a woman? Do you understand, for instance, that foreplay should start the *week* before? It's no good being truly thrilling about half an hour before the act. 'A standing prick has no conscience,' a man once explained to me. A woman does like to feel she's *liked*. You're not always that convincing.

Sorry I spoke

By the way, personally speaking, I have no complaints about you once I'm *in* bed. Maybe I was lucky, but you've been terrific. It's one of the few places where men and women can be equal. Oh, did I love being equal in the best of all occupations! What do you mean, I must have some complaints? I was really warming up there.... Well, since you brought it up, I do have a complaint about the way you get *out* of bed. I mean, who *are* you the next morning, that stranger who jackknifes out of bed the moment he wakes up, so determined to get on with his day? I have to go to work too. But I wouldn't dream of leaving a bed that had you in it with what can only be described as indecent haste. Great lovers are tender in the morning. That's often the bit the woman remembers when she thinks about you during the day. Do you find it hard to be tender? Are you suppressing emotions or don't you have any? It puzzles me that considering the fuss you men make about sex, not enough of you abandon yourselves to the total pleasure of being with a woman. Intimacy is for everyone with a soul, not just for gorgeous men in the after-shave ads.

Sometimes I think I've had sex with men and romance with women. Well, not in every case. But when a women says, 'I love you,' it's often a decision she's come to about you. She has 'fallen in love' and she goes on loving. For years, in some cases. When you say 'I love you,' it seems to mean 'Here and now, at this moment, I feel something for you.' It doesn't mean that you will feel the same by next Wednesday. I agree that it's better than nothing. D'you know a masseuse once told me that she can always tell when a woman is having a great love affair – she has absolutely no sign of tension in her back. But a man can bare his back and his heart about a wonderful woman in his life and his back can still be knotted with tension. Yes, I know I have educated thumbs. I'll massage you in a minute. How come I'm always the one doing the massaging?

Do you know that it isn't too terrible to occasionally *plan* a date? You're at the top of my list of things to do, but as I have a full and funny life apart from you, it would help to *know* when I was going to see you. Dorothy Parker said, 'All your life you wait around for some damned man.' You do seem to expect me to give up a great deal. What do you

Sorry I spoke

mean, 'One of us has to make sacrifices'? Why me? Couldn't we both give up a bit of our lives? Why do we mostly see *your* friends? I like them, but they chose you. It's really odd that you don't like more of my women friends. Couldn't you just make a little effort to get to know them? Women always have to try to be nice to your friends and business associates. Part of the supportive role. Which reminds me, that man in the foyer at work the other day was *not* a hot date. He's the vice-president of the company, and you needn't have been so offhand with him. A woman would never dream of behaving like that.

Why are you so secretive? Why can't you easily say what you do on the nights we don't see each other? Why don't your friends have names? You say, 'I'm busy Thursday,' or 'I have to have a drink with someone.' You invite curiosity. I mean, if you can't even share the unimportant details, what hope do I have that you'll share bigger things? Do you really think I mind which Tom, Dick or Charlotte you're seeing? Come to that, why do you *volunteer* lies? When I'm happily minding my own business, you'll tell me that you have to see your ex-wife, and I mumble, 'That's nice.' But of course I'm annoyed when you're seen in the theatre instead. I don't see why the truth is so distasteful to you. I find it so much easier. And why do you say things you don't mean? Why do you say 'Let's see a movie this week' or tell me you're getting tickets for the opera? I didn't *ask* to be invited out by you. But once you've invited me out, I do notice when you don't call.

What do you *really* think when a woman phones you? Do you think she's desperate or just being friendly? I know it depends on the woman. Perhaps we should have made a list in the early days of what pleased you and what pleased me. Ten conditions of an affair: I love flowers, being telephoned, fussed over, being encouraged, and constructively criticized. What do *you* love? Can't the massage wait a few minutes? Why do I think we're having a discussion when you think we're having an argument? I do wish you wouldn't say 'One day I'll tell you.' What's wrong with now? Why do men rarely say the things they're feeling at the time? Why does it sometimes take years for you to say 'I was so much in love with you' or 'You really hurt me'? I wish you'd recognize at the time when a good thing's on to you.

Sorry I spoke

By the way, have I ever told you that men don't really age better than women? I mean, Robert Redford would make a lousy fifty-five-year old woman. It's just that a woman can accept lines and crow's feet in a man. Men can be so judgmental about the way a woman looks. 'She's aged badly,' they say. What the hell does that mean? You want us to retain the bland good looks of our youth, but you don't apply the same standards to yourselves. Oh, and I'm sick of men who tell me they used to date a woman 'who looked just like Catherine Deneuve' or who had 'a truly amazing body'. Not that I suppose you told them at the time, either. Do you care what women want. Do you understand their needs and simply not feel like fulfilling them?

Is it easier to pretend you don't know what we're talking about? No, I don't know where *The Economist* is. I did *not* hide it. D'you know that I sometimes feel closest to you sharing the most trivial things? I love shopping in the supermarket with you, love riding in the car when you're relaxed and touching my leg. It's so nice that you came with me to buy a pair of shoes, and when you picked me up at the hairdresser's, I was almost weak with affection for you. When we're out for an evening, however good it is, often the best part is the postmortem with you afterward. You and me laughing over coffee. And then falling into bed as tired friends.

Did I ever tell you that I love you for your weaknesses as much as for your strengths? Financial success isn't everything, you know. I think success is happy. What's better than happy? You know, it's the man who can make a relationship work. Even the most difficult or resistant women can usually be brought around to succumbing to the pleasures of loving and committing. But however hard a woman tries, there's little she can do to convince a reluctant man. He may stay with her because it's easy for him. Unconditional love. But she's insecure every inch of the way. How often are men insecure in relationships with women?

Do you think love is mostly about timing? You do? I know there's also a time to sleep. I do remember you have to leave at 8:30 a.m. No, I haven't forgotten about your back.

I'd like to tell you that despite everything, I do love you. But that might complicate things. Maybe I do understand you better than you

Sorry I spoke

think, but I'd be a fool if I accepted everything totally without comment.

Do I really have an amazing body? You're not just saying that? Yes, I'll go and get the baby oil right this minute. Shoulders? Neck? Lower spine? *This* is your favourite thing in the world? Well, I'm glad we spoke. It always helps to know what you want.

Women

This could be the end of something small

*W*hat am I doing here? How much wine did I drink? Do I have any codeine? Did last night really happen? Isn't the back of his neck vulnerable? Aren't his shoulders nice and masculine? What do I mean nice? Is he sleeping as deeply as it sounds? Did we say anything embarrassing to each other? Is he moving? Will he wake up? Shouldn't I creep to the bathroom? What do I look like? Why wasn't I more prepared? Doesn't my mouth taste awful? Can I slide out of this bed without waking him? Will he open an eye and see me? Why aren't I more confident of my body? Will I wobble as I walk. Why was I so anti-exercise? Why didn't I go on a diet? Does it really matter at this point? Why didn't I sleep on the side near my clothes? What are my suede trousers doing on the window-sill? Why don't I go to the bathroom now? Did he stir? Which door is it? Why wasn't that door marked 'Cupboard'? Who designed this room? Did he hear the door click? Can he hear me? Do I flush the lavatory and wake him up unromantically or do I act like a charming slut? Does he like sluts? Whose toothbrushes are these. Does he have guest toothbrushes? What is that bottle of Chanel 19 doing there? Does he still see her? Is she good in bed? Is she good out of bed? What am I thinking about? Why isn't the hot water working? Where's the Nivea? How do you regulate these damned taps? What do you put on a scald? Shall I wash everywhere? Did I imagine he'd have a bidet? Isn't baby powder a nice touch of innocence? What's he doing with it? Don't I look rather good, considering? Don't my eyes have a certain shine? Shall I use his razor? Aren't my

This could be the end of something small

legs a little rough? Will he be mad if I use his razor? Will he notice if I've
used it? Isn't it a relief I had my hair washed yesterday. Does he like tits?
Can I get back into bed without him noticing? Shall I douse myself with
Chloé or is that too terribly obvious? How high is this room? Why does
he keep that photograph of his ex-wife and baby on the walnut chest? Is
she a natural red-head? Isn't that baby about 12 years old now? Does my
stomach look flatter when I'm lying on my back? What'll we do when
he wakes up? Will I get to like him? Does he have plans for any part of
this weekend? Will this ruin a friendship? Do I need a lover? Can I cope
with one? Will he rush out of bed to play tennis at nine o'clock? Will he
drive me home, leave the engine running and say 'I'll be in touch'? Why
don't I go now and leave a note saying 'This could be the end of
something small'?

Does he always sleep this soundly? Is he really turning over and
smiling with his eyes closed? Will the men delivering my new sofa be
livid if I'm not in my flat? Isn't it good to have this arm thrown gently
over me? Isn't it wonderful it's starting to rain? What else can he find to
do in this weather? Do I care about Chanel 19? Or where my boots are?
Or if I'm slightly overweight? Shall I wake him? Or is he going to sleep
till lunchtime because *he* can't face the morning after?

Celibacy

$\mathcal{I}$ think that being celibate
Is *not* a cause to celebrate
It's not a state I ever sought
It's merely a disease I caught.

Truly I am most surprised,
the illness isn't recognised.
There're thousands in the same dilemma
Who never feel a sexual tremor.

No sex please, the modern credo,
where on earth is my libido?
Farewell days of lustful greed,
the less you have the less you need.

Was it the contraceptive pill
that made a generation ill?
Or have we sadly overdosed
on the thing that we liked most?

It seems that in the USA
'celibate' is chic today.
What the hell is New York doing
isn't anybody screwing?

Can't the medical profession
cure this negative obsession?
I might as well become a nun
oh fruitless nineteen-eighty-one.

Celibacy

We're in a sexual perplexia
on a par with anorexia.
February '80 was the last time
I enjoyed my favourite pastime.

What will become of thee and me
can we live on memory?
Hope to hell that we pull through it,
I've forgotten how to do it.

Valerie's confession

He's a sonovabitch
But he's terribly rich
And frankly we live awfully well.
I'm not happy, of course
But who'd want a divorce?
Without money life's utterly hell.

I spend *sans arrêt*
I go shopping each day
That's the best bit of being his wife.
Yes I'm often depressed
But I'm very well dressed
And I've not looked so good in my life.

Oh I shan't be a bore
But I've clothes you'd kill for
Thank God for American Express
I buy things I don't need
Out of boredom and greed
And to show that I married success.

Sure my old friends may laugh
But I *like* having staff
In the homes that we have here and there.
So – our sex life is dead
But there's money instead
I'm so numb now I really don't care.

Valerie's confession

I mean – where would I go
if I leave? I don't know
how you manage alone in this town.
I'm a legalised whore
But it's better than poor
I would die if my standards went down.

So I shop and I drink
And I try not to think
That my life's a charade and a mess.
No, I'm set in this track
And there's no going back
from the life of a Jewish princess.

I know

I know how to make him happy
I am sexy, warm and zappy.
Confident was I about my lover.
But there is the glaring factor
that he's left me for an actor.
Do you think that given time
I will recover?

Fear of flirting

*A*s everyone knows, all interaction between a man and a woman is now virtually impossible. It's been proved time and time again that it simply doesn't work. But ages ago, before society owned up to this fact – I mean, I'm talking way back before the Great Emotional Famine – there was a lot of flirting about. It may seem extraordinary to you, but that's the way we were.

Men and women were joky with each other. They'd wink and grin and say '*Vive la différence*' and smile at each other across crowded rooms. Flirting was a kind of promissory note of what might happen if all things were possible. An 'I'm very good at it and I'd *love* to do it with you' wicked look. That was flirting.

Listen. What did we know? We gave a come-hither smile and played with a broken shoulder strap – forgive me, we did sink that low – and the men came thither. Who knew they were all sexist pigs? Some of them looked like male chauvinist lambs. My consciousness was in my cleavage, where I also kept a tiny ball of cotton wool soaked in Arpège. Promise them anything. I used to deliver when I was in love. We were all too dumb to realise how *political* it all was. It's amazing how we survived to become the happy, fulfilled, *aware* women we are today. You just can't imagine what we went through. And what we *did*. And how we were *treated*. You know, we actually used to *dress* to *please* men sometimes. We looked interested when they spoke to us, allowed them to *hold* us close when we danced and we just stood there and *took it* when a man said 'You've got a great body.' Who knew? We spent *ages* getting ready to go out because there might be men 'there', we wore clothes that plainly showed we had waists and tits and hips, and we thought celibacy was a disease, not an aspiration. Can you credit that?

Fear of flirting

I'm afraid we were so unspeakably female we even flirted with our *legs*. We'd cross 'em in our 10-denier tights so that men could see our shapely calves and perfect ankles and high-heeled shoes. And I have to own up. I used to curl my lashes before the mascara application so that I could do a more frivolous class of wink. This alone could disbar me from the sisterhood if the knowledge became public.

We were fools. We were so utterly pre-sperm bank about life in general and men in particular.... Oh, and where flirting *led*. You've no idea of the downright patronising behaviour and belittling of women to which we were subjected. If you smiled back at a man, teased him in a conversational sort of way and maybe touched his arm, next thing you knew the manipulative bugger would take *full* advantage of the situation and ask you out for dinner and the theatre. And *he'd* pay. I mean, the arrogance of assuming that you couldn't pay for yourself.

We didn't know any better. We let them get away with it. They'd open the car door to let you in then close it again leaving you *trapped* while they walked around and got in their side. You'd get to the restaurant and they'd open the door yet again. They seemed to assume you didn't have the strength to do it for yourself. And once you got inside, the table for two was always booked in *his* name. *Your* name didn't matter, that was obvious. Invariably the restaurant was owned by a *man* and if you ate Italian style you'd have to endure comments like *'bella signora'* from those bloody sexist Italian waiters. They never commented on the *man's* appearance. He wouldn't have stood for it, would he? It was only women who were meant to be physically attractive to *men*.

The whole thing was outrageous. But we were unaware of what was happening to us. Too caught up in it all to see how we were being controlled. During the days when I flirted and was being flirted with I was so politically naïve that I allowed men to take me away on luxury holidays. I mean that's how stupid I was. But, you know, I was starting to notice.... For instance, I spotted that on every occasion there was a *man* piloting the plane. Don't tell me a 747 or the occasional small helicopter is *that* difficult to operate. There were *men* carrying your cases, *men* waiting at table and beach *boys* fixing your rum punches

Fear of flirting

while you stretched out daft and still flirting on the Caribbean sand.

It was a conspiracy, of course. A huge international male conspiracy to keep you sexually interested in men. Huh! No wonder men like the idea of flirting. In those days the bastards would stop at nothing. They'd pour champagne down your throat, tell you you were wonderful, drone on endlessly about how much they liked being with you and how they'd positively *melted*. They'd say 'I love you', talk of children and then. And *then*. Manipulative to the bloody end they'd ask you to live with them or *marry* them. I mean, enough is enough. Who did they think we were? Flirting? That's where flirting led. Thank God you're too young to remember. And thank God my generation saw through it for what it was. Where *would* we be today if that sort of male behaviour had been allowed to continue? Can you imagine?

So where do we go, girls?

*W*ell, *hello.* I was just about to 'phone *you.* You've been *thinking?* Gosh, what else is new? *You* keep wondering what we're supposed to be doing with our lives? You and everyone I know. Well, apart from Jeffrey and Aline who've just had Joshua. Jeffrey said he's amazing and he supposes they'll be 'nesting' for a bit. I suppose 'nesting' must be rather nice. You can stay in and gaze at this wondrous new person you've produced and feel deep down contented about life in its true meaning and you can plan a future for him or her. What do you mean, 'And how long does contented last?' I'm just saying it must be nice for a bit. Well, exactly. They've made a *decision* about something. I don't know why we don't make decisions. No, it is hard for single women to know if they're doing the right thing. I agree with you – parenting *doesn't* seem to be a shared experience and women do seem to end up doing most of the work.

Don't even *ask* me where we'd fit a child into our lives. It's just that I've noticed that everyone seems to be having them lately. Look, I *know* children don't *solve* anything. Yes, I realise that you have a different set of problems. But maybe it's good to have a different set of problems. Men are getting nicer and more *aware* about kids. I think they'd *like* to share more. Of *course*, I wonder about not having children. Maybe we will regret it, maybe we won't. That's true – couples without children often have better relationships. Well, statistically speaking they do seem to stay married longer and all that. But who knows?

Look, I'd be absolutely *thrilled* if I had a daughter of about seven

So where do we go, girls?

years old right now. I was only thinking that when we were in Skiathos last May. And I'm weak for Bonnie's son Brad. I mean I adore him. He's practically edible. All those freckles and that shiny hair. I'd have loved a son like him. I *know* she's divorced, but it's fairly amicable. Look, I *know* people with the most adorable kids in the world still get divorced. No, I'm *not* aiming at being a single parent family. No, I'm *not* saying I want a friendly divorce. Look, I had more in mind a friendly marriage or whatever. But she does have those perfect sons for the rest of her life. No, I *wouldn't* like to have led her life because honestly I'd have hated to have been married young. It suits some people, it doesn't suit others.

Well, I'm like you really. I kept thinking there was loads to do with life and there was always something better around the corner. There was. I mean give or take a few tricky moments. OK, there were lots of tricky moments. But you're not going to get me to say I didn't enjoy it all because I did. You know I really liked the men I've known. Deeply loved a couple of them. But you're right. I didn't really picture them as husbands or fathers. I don't know why. I just didn't. Sure, we *talked* about it. I've probably spent years negotiating with men, now I come to think about it. But two people have to want the same thing at the same time and I'm not terrifically good at synchronising. Listen, negotiating was fun. Yes, it does sound a bit silly today. I know, I know. Times have changed suddenly. You don't have to tell *me* that. Yes, I probably did think that marriage dulls the senses. Maybe I still do. But you're right. Security does seem to be more appealing than it used to. It's something to do with the 'Eighties isn't it? And sex? Oh God, yes. It's probably got a lot to do with sex.

Don't ask me what we're supposed to be doing about it. I'm still trying to adjust. I mean all those days of meeting a new man, finding him exciting, talking endlessly, all that getting to know you stuff and then one day you end up in bed. I mean all that's down the drain isn't it? Can you *imagine* asking someone his recent sexual history in great detail, saying you can't tolerate casual sexual behaviour on account of it's a health hazard? And then you have to wait while he struggles into a condom which you'd better have by your bedside in case he's come unprepared.

So where do we go, girls?

I'm not crazy and paranoid. I tell you it's come to that. I'm just so stunned by all this talk of AIDS that I don't find the thought of sex as attractive as I used to. No, you're right – I'll probably recover. Of *course*, the figures mean that there are millions of men who don't have the AIDS virus. Yes, I suppose you can always get tested. Well, that's true. The good part is we will be totally *repelled* by men who are anything less than faithful and caring. Keep reminding me I said that.

Mind you, it could be rather nice if things got back to the way they were 30 years ago. We could do flirting, heavy petting, all that. Could be fun. Don't be daft. You could 'go all the way' when you knew who you were dealing with and if he had a clean bill of health. Oh it's just a thought. OK, OK, it would take men a little time to get used to the idea. But you know I had lunch with this man a few days ago and he's been married for three years. *Yes*, he's attractive. About mid-thirties I think. No, as a matter of fact she's five years *older* than him. I don't *know* where she found him. People meet. Of *course* there are attractive, available men around. Well he didn't come flying through the window of her flat while she was dripping around thinking about the meaning of life and should she do some ironing. I think they met through work. Or at a cocktail party or something. Yes, she is rather high-powered.

Anyway. What I was trying to say is *he* said that if he were single today he'd think twice about having affairs. He also said that a lot more men these days would rather have one special person than play around. Well of course it's partly an age thing but it's also a sign of the times don't you think? You know, security. Making a decision and getting on with life. Yes, masses of people I know are in monogamous relationships. It's true that in some cases they just drifted in but these days they don't show much sign of drifting out.

Yes it *is* funny about people living together who are screechingly against marriage. I don't really understand why they're so dead against it. It's a sort of open door policy. You know, if the world outside shows some signs of improvement they might just leave. If they *happened* to meet someone else and all that. Well, *obviously* the tax allowance on mortgages doesn't exactly encourage you to marry if you're both working hard and earning quite a bit. I suppose property is important. I mean

So where do we go, girls?

it *is*. You know, now I get up at seven every morning and jog around the park it's really hit me. I *know* I'm anti-exercise but I'm pro fresh air and oxygen. Honestly I feel great running for half an hour. I so love Kensington Gardens and the round pond and the geese and the people walking their dogs and other joggers. Running gets your endorphins going or something and I have time to think.

Well, no, what *hits* me is those houses and flats with the 'For Sale' signs on the way to the park. And I keep thinking, should I be moving? Yes property prices drive me *crazy*. It's barely worth going out to work. You should just keep doing up properties and selling them. I agree I'm sick of hearing people talking about how much their flats are worth. Do you remember when we used to talk about *relationships*? Now it's all work and should you buy or sell a flat.

Stop with the, 'Are we working too hard?' We're working too hard. But everyone I know who has a job is working till they drop. It's bloody fear of downward mobility. No, come on. We *do* enjoy it. Yes I admit it takes up too much time. Well, maybe you *would* be happier with a less pressurised job. Well, it *might* be healthier to live in the country. But you hate the country. OK I'm exaggerating. But you do get bored there after a couple of days. All right, so you'd get used to it. OK, you'd be really relaxed and more at peace and less exhausted. But what would you *do*? I'm not being negative. But I just can't see you giving up a terrific salary and your flat to go and buy a thatched cottage and help run a tea shop in a village. I don't know why. I just can't. Don't say, 'So what's the solution to this exhausting life?' How would I know? Try running in the morning. Look, Marta says you can have peace in the grave. We're in prime time living right now.

Well currently I'm wondering if we should make more of an effort with men. You know, find a bit more time for them. Yes, indeed, *find* them. We hardly ever entertain on the grounds we're too busy and we're dreadful at making plans. I've got a card someone once sent me which says, 'The reason things aren't going to plan is there never was a plan.' I mean we've got flats and we earn money and we could easily give dinner parties or ask people around for drinks or Sunday brunch. Why don't we? Yes I *know* it means making a decision. I *know* we already know

So where do we go, girls?

men but the ones I know are either past lovers or best friends. We're not *seizing* hold of life, are we? I don't know why I said that. I must have read it somewhere. But you know, I do feel we should be a bit more socially *active* apart from work. I guess we'll simply have to *make* time. Look, it's no good saying the ideal thing would be a marvellous man you keep in a cupboard who would pop out when you need him. Don't say your damned Filofax is so full you wouldn't have time to go through 'all that'. We're sounding as pressurised and crazy as all the men we used to criticise.

Look, I keep meeting rather nice men who say they'd *like* a relationship. No, I don't think they're just saying that. No, it's *not* merely about compromising. It's about facing reality. OK, I admit reality hasn't been my strong point. Yes, I might well be sounding like a reformed alcoholic. I *know* I haven't even found the time to have my sofas covered. Well I've been going out a lot lately. And I'd rather go to the theatre and dinner parties and roll around Covent Garden and crash at that wonderful crêperie than think about the sofas. OK I *know* I keep seeing people I already know. But sometimes I meet new ones. Look, I'm trying to reach an objective bit by bit. I started going out because I thought I was working too hard and not enjoying myself enough. Now I'm working and playing and loving London all of a sudden. Well, it could apply to a teenager in her first job. Give me a break. I'm trying to sort things out. Sometimes you have to take a step back to take three forward. Men are next, silly. I'm due to fall in love again. You're right, we both are. God, everyone I know is except my married friends. We'll all have to stop being so emotionally corseted. No I don't necessarily think that eager and enthusiastic sounds like desperate. I suppose I mean that you just have to show nice men that there is room for them in your life. And that you need them and want them. Don't say we used to *do* all that. We obviously haven't been doing it recently.

Look, I don't *know* how I'm going to rig falling in love again. But I'm going to bear it in mind. Sort of expose myself to the possibility. So you've been exposing yourself and nothing has been happening? Well, it could take a little longer. I don't know. As long as it takes. Not *all* the marvellous interesting men like dumb pretty women. And come on.

So where do we go, girls?

They're not *all* gay. You don't need to bring that up. I count that as an unfortunate but ultimately interesting time of my life. He was merely exercising his options. So what do we do? As I see it, we can either sell our flats or stay put. Go out and meet men or stay in. Change our jobs or stay where we are. Lose weight or go for the new fuller rounded look. Move in with the men we already know or they could move in again with us. Go on living the way we are and see what happens. And I might grow my hair and start doing sit-ups. I mean what's so good about now is we're spoilt rotten for choice when you think about it. You just have to *decide* what you want to do and then do it.

Look, I'll cope with the AIDS problem when I decide on the man. I'll opt for safer sex with the safest person. Yes, this talk's helped me, too. Yes, I *have* thought about the question of priorities. And I have come to a big decision. I have *definitely* decided to have my sofas covered.

Undercover lovers

As a hostess I am frightful
yet I often get requests
from some girlfriends quite delightful
who just love to be my guests.

Well of course they all adore me
I have never doubted that
but what they want's the front door key
to my walk-up penthouse flat.

They don't keep fit or do knee bends
yet they leap the eighty stairs
they're my very married girlfriends
who are having love affairs.

As I'm sexually inactive
being single and confused
it's romantic and attractive
that my bed is being used.

I get notes left under covers
thanking me for the champagne
funny messages from lovers
asking may they come again.

Used to pity the poor housewife
but I've sadly been deluded.
For true romance *and* a sex life
first get married I've concluded.

Cupboard loves

My wardrobe is a diary
of all the days that used to be.
Nothing there is 'mixed' or 'matched'
but I'm pathetically attached
to clothes I know I'll never wear
nostalgically I keep them there ...

All thrown together in a mess
the story of my life I guess.
Boots collapsed upon the floor
strappy shoes I never wore.
Dresses from my sluttish phase
je ne sais quoi for 'special' days.

The Ascot hat my friends still borrow,
the jersey dress that clung in sorrow
as a love affair was ending ...
My Turnbull shirts whose cuffs need mending.
A sparkling plunge from someone's sale,
to win back a retreating male.

A fur coat to watch *football* in.
The size 4 dress – *he* liked me thin.
Underwear from Janet Reger?
The classic camel coat from Jaeger
which proved to be an awful bore
just like the man I bought it for.

Cupboard loves

The see-through jump suit flower-like pressed
between a raincoat and a vest.
(Vests, I read are coming back
I'll never ever wear the mac).
That jump suit was a New York hit,
I couldn't bear to part with it.

Clothes I chose with tender care
for someone special who was 'there'.
It matters not the men are gone
for some brief span I turned 'em on.
A lover now I couldn't face
the fact is there's no wardrobe space.

Guilt-free sloth

I don't know how you feel about it but I think that life for most of us today is stressful. And stress can lead to heart disease and heart disease can lead to death and Lord knows where that can lead. It does seem obvious that a person should, if possible, try to avoid going down that particular route and you can do that by eliminating stage one. Better than that, you should be taking strong anti-stress measures. One excellent way of doing this is to do nothing whenever you can. Yes, you read it right. *Do nothing.* Consider the positive benefits of being an underachiever in your spare time.

Curiously enough, most women are very bad at doing nothing. The possibility of 'benefits' to be derived from total relaxation doesn't seem to have occurred to them. They read about all the things women are meant to be accomplishing these days and they spend every minute of every hour of their free time *doing.* They feel they have to use every last ounce of energy improving their bodies, their minds, their homes or their social lives. They're rushing out to tennis lessons, hurrying to psychology classes, feverishly tidying or re-decorating already respect-able homes, cooking unnecessary meals for casual friends or they're flopped out in a heap after a strenuous aerobics class.

To 'go for it' is a terrific idea. But all the time? What about to 'go *with* it'? To succumb to the passing urge to flop down on the sofa, to stay at home and watch TV or to crawl into bed with a mug of tea and the evening paper?

As an ex-hell-bent self-improver and gadabout, I can only describe to you the blissful and relaxing delights of 'letting go'. Stopping. It's so e-a-s-y, so unwinding, so bloody marvellous to cease competing with yourself and everyone else. These days I'm as contented as a newly fed

Guilt-free sloth

budgerigar pottering around – doing nothing. People haven't pointed at me because I've gained four pounds in weight and haven't read the Sunday papers. No one has stopped calling because I left the washing up in the sink.

Of course I have spent time experimenting with big stuff like putting my hair up and moving flowers from one end of the terrace to the other. And I almost read a Germaine Greer book. I do browse through *Zest* and one of these days I'll write away for one of those track suits. My friend Jo tells me about her conditioning classes and Elaine keeps me regularly in touch with her home improvements. Frankly I don't know what I'd do without all my super-dynamic friends. Most of them accomplish more than enough for two people so I don't feel at all bad about doing nothing.

That, according to Dr Margaret Reinhold, a well-known London psychiatrist, is the main problem. Women feel *guilty* doing nothing. Dr Reinhold pointed out that Sigmund Freud was convinced that women are born masochists. And a lot of women out there are proving him right.

'When,' she sighed, 'will women learn to cherish themselves? Self-love and self-pampering go hand in hand. There's everything right with spending the afternoon lying peacefully on a soft sofa, sipping high-calorie drinks and reading the glossy magazines. If a woman is able to recline happily on a pile of comfortable cushions instead of rushing guiltily around feeling she has to *achieve* something, she can be said to have reached emotional maturity and got rid of her masochistic tendencies.'

Perhaps I can pass on to you a few tips about how to achieve this particular aspect of emotional maturity. I'm very grown up in this area. All the activities I suggest are guaranteed stress-free and there's also very little forward planning involved.

1 Potter. Wander from one room to another. You can touch things. Pull out a couple of books. Turn lamp bases upside down to see if the price is still on them. Potter around near your wardrobe. Pull out a few clothes. Consider if the little red numero will still be wearable this autumn. Try on a couple of sweaters and see if they still go with your grey flannel

Guilt-free sloth

trousers. Consider a belt. Try a scarf or two. On no account attempt a sort-out. That counts as activity and is not part of pottering.

2 Ponder. Think about funny or tender moments in your life. Ponder on whether to wear bright red nail varnish or to stay with the Dior transparent glaze. Consider whether the television set in the living room would look better in the bedroom. Ponder on whether to move the seriously sprouting green pot plant. Ask yourself how it manages to look so healthy when you never speak to it. Ponder on how long you can go on using the Man Size Kleenex in the bathroom and tell yourself that tomorrow you will buy at least four blue lavatory rolls. (NB *tomorrow* is the key word here.) It is firmly against the Relaxed Pondering rules to think about why your relationships haven't worked out, why he hasn't called for a week and if you're going to be able to meet 'someone' in time to have children.

3 Plunge into a cream bath or a bubble bath. You could ponder for 10 minutes deciding which. Have a self-love splurge and buy yourself half a bottle of champagne and to this add some freshly squeezed orange juice. Sip this slowly while reclining in the bath. Or take a warm, loving shower and immediately you're dry, flop out on the bed. Cover yourself in body lotion.

4 Pass out. This simple little feat can be accomplished in many parts of your home. On the sofa, on the floor, on the bed, in front of the television, in the bath and at the dining table. It's best done alone because research has shown that a greater degree of relaxation is achieved if you don't have to wake up and explain what you're doing and why. Beginners in the gentle art of passing out should lie still in their chosen position and allow their upper eyelids slowly to touch their lower lids. Think of your mind as a cluttered room; carefully vacuum out all your thoughts.

5 Preen. Get out all your make-up. The eyeshadows, blushers, lipsticks, mascara, cleansers, toners, gold glitz and scrub cream. Cleanse your face thoroughly and then start to experiment. Try a lash comb and separate your lashes when you've mascaraed them. Try brushing your hair into different styles. Stop the *moment* you're tiring, scrunch your hair off your face and give yourself a lemon face pack. Rest on the bed with the phone off the hook until the pack has dried.

Guilt-free sloth

6 Phone. Make sure you're wearing your most comfortable clothes; lie back on the sofa and call friends. Don't call anyone with a serious and interminable 'problem' you may be called on to solve. Try a person who's recently been on holiday or is not getting divorced. It's more restful to listen than to talk so say 'Tell me about everything that's been happening to you'. Call back again the next day and apologise for falling asleep.

7 Pick up a really good book. Not a heavy one. You're not to strain yourself in any way. Paperbacks are best. Make a pot of fresh tea or coffee on a tray, put a flower in a small vase on the tray and then curl up in your favourite chair and read for a couple of hours.

8 Procrastinate. If you don't know where to begin – don't. Stay in bed, preferably till lunchtime. It's one of the safest, softest places in the world. And bed rest is an excellent tonic for a busy woman. You may have to exercise real will-power not to get up but do fight any achievement urges you may have while practising this vital relaxation exercise.

9 Prance about. If you're feeling frisky, put on a good tape and dance around the flat. With any luck the frisky mood will give way to one of sudden tiredness and you can fall on the sofa again and put your feet up on the coffee table.

10 Play with jewellery, sort through old photographs. Sit back with a heap of old letters, diaries and pictures and remember when. Sort through your box of junk jewellery and try on the gold hoop earrings and the brassy sparkly one you wore to that party in the spring.

11 Play with a friend. Not nearly enough people go out to play these days. Invite someone around who'll collapse on the sofa and watch three re-runs of *Cheers* or who'll take a stroll to the park with a kite. Maybe let him/her go for a stroll and come back and tell you how it was. Plan a joint party you're going to give in the summer of '88. Keep the guest list flexible. Discuss why Clive James has sex appeal.

12 Put pen to paper. Start writing a letter to your best girl friend in Florida, Chipping Sodbury or wherever. On no account attempt to finish this letter at one sitting.

13 STOP THINKING ABOUT WHAT YOU SHOULD BE DOING. Resist all attempts by friends to get you involved in some

Guilt-free sloth

activity. Do not be pressurised in any way. It's good and positive to answer 'absolutely nothing' in answer to that damnfool eternal question 'What are you doing this weekend?' You do *not* need to go to a party with everyone at work, your stomach will *not* become a mound of overnight flab if you miss your Saturday exercise class. So *what* if your kitchen cupboards stay in the same muddle for another week? You, the Hoover, the washing up liquid, the oven, the Nautilus equipment and the Linguaphone Tape in conversational Turkish deserve a rest. In a future article the topic for discussion may well be 'What price emotional maturity?' Should any reader encounter any relationship problems arising from this new leisure lifestyle, they should write to Irma Kurtz. Don't write to me. I shall be on the sofa pondering if and when tomorrow comes I'll have the energy to clear up the incredible mess.

Hemmed in by love

*A*re you alone? Can you speak?
Oh, that's great. Seems like ages since we talked. You're exhausted?
Took me all my energy to dial your number. No, I know we didn't used
to be this tired. But we're working hard. And you're travelling some
weeks. I know it's not just that. Coming out and saying it are you? Oh
God, what a relief to talk to you. You mean it's not just me? I'm not just
imagining it? You mean it *is* difficult having a full time man around?
Honestly you're finding it difficult? Me too. Life is getting impossible.
No, I *know* he's wonderful. I'm not disputing their wonderfulness.
Especially when you think what's around out there. But how do we
make it through a working week and keep ourselves together and find
the time to be terrific to them? You work all day and see someone all
night – what do we expect?

No, I don't get to talk to anybody any more either. Well, rarely.
Deprived? I'm practically psychotic. I loved all those phone calls and
chat. Oh, of course some of the calls were time-wasting. I know that.
But they were part of my life. Oh don't. Don't even ask why a man and
most of your friends don't mix. I don't think he'd object if I insisted. But
it's such an effort to go through an evening with people who don't know
or care about each other and are being pleasant for your sake. Honestly,
at this point I'd rather see them separately. No by the time I'm home at
seven thirty I'm not too thrilled at the thought of seeing *his* friends. I
agree it's awful. Oh, you've tried giving the little dinner parties have
you? Well, no wonder you're tired of cooking. No, I know you never
get paid back for the cost of the meal and the wine, even if it is his friends.
You're so good. I don't even try. He loves Marks and Spencer's ready
cooked and he knows baked beans are good for him. Honestly, he's so

Hemmed in by love

appreciative and easy to please. Yes, it is nice being loved. Sure we earned it. No, I didn't know it was going to be like this. I never know how anything is going to be. It's a change. I remember reading somewhere that all change is traumatic.

Perhaps this is what security feels like. No, it is very unsettling. I don't know if it is going to suit me either. Perhaps insecurity suited us? I agree I'm too tired to analyse it. D'you know I fell asleep at that little French place off the Fulham Road last Thursday. Of *course* I don't have the time to *do* anything. I mean you can't with a man constantly around, can you? They take up space and you have to talk to them and find out what they want to do and if they want to eat. You can't just leave them sitting there while you get on with things, can you? Daphné says Ian practically follows her from room to room. She has to put up a good case for 20 minutes to herself while she takes a bath. No, I'm behind with everything. My wardrobe's a mess, it needs a thorough sort out. There are endless things that need doing. He's not seriously interested in the flat, except as the setting for where he sees me. But were men ever? Oh, it's the letters I should write, the bills I should pay. Expenses, insurance claims. Light bulbs, plugs. I mean you have to keep up a flat, don't you? He's obsessive about *his* house. Don't agree with me. I'd like to be wrong. Yes, it *is* marvellous to have the whole evening to yourself. I'm revelling in it, too. What I'm finding so difficult is that before you *knew* you were free unless you had a date. Now you're busy every night of the week unless you can think of a reason for being alone. I mean, I can't make out a decent case for being by myself. I just miss it. We did get so used to it didn't we? Do you remember how much we used to *do*? And *talk*? Oh God, they were such funny times, weren't they? People dropping in at odd hours and coming to stay and shopping at weekends and those silly lunches when we just threw everyone together because it didn't matter. Pottering? You miss that? Oh, me too. I ache to potter.

Those do-nothing times we used to have. Dripping around, you used to call it. No, I can't understand it either. I'm as confused as hell. Yes, I *know* this is what we wanted. Nice warm, intelligent, loving men we care about. Of course we love them. What do you mean, another of life's little jokes? Well, I've been thinking maybe we'd got one thing wrong.

Hemmed in by love

Listen, you know how we'd figured that if you were happy and self-contained and pleased with your life single then it would be simple to live with a partner? We were wrong. Sure we managed to *attract* them on the grounds that we weren't desperate. But I get the feeling that we were so happy and all that *because* we were free. Of *course* I don't know what we do about it. No, I *wouldn't* like the pain again. Oh God, how did we live through all that? No, apart from the pain it was very good.

Well, obviously it's irritating to have someone around you constantly. No, I can't say that finding the lavatory seat up every time I go in there creates that much conflict. But it is funny that they never think to put it back the way it was when they went in, isn't it? Well, yes, couples are boring. They always were, unless you knew them both very well separately. Don't tell *me* you have different sorts of conversations. I know it. I loathe the fact that you can't ask someone an intimate question. I mean even a funny question and get a decent answer. It's all that light, bright, amusing stuff with the occasional political foray. All that gossip about people you know and restaurants you've eaten in and what's in the bloody newspapers. Not one honest moment.

Anti-social? You can say that again. I think you could describe me as socially hostile. Listen, when do you get the chance even in a single life to service the friendships you've already *made*? I mean unless someone dies I can't take on any new people. Growing up? You think this is what it's about? I think you're probably right. No, of course I'm not sure. It is time we made an effort. I agree. We *do* have to change some time. Take responsibility for someone other than ourselves. I know it was easier before. Yes, this is worthwhile. Isn't it what life's supposed to be all about? No, I'm too tired to make a big effort.

You know, my problem is that I don't yet know how to tread that fine line which means I have enough space to myself and yet there's still togetherness. I mean, the other Sunday there I was lying in bed, talking about space. *Me* needing space. I couldn't believe I was saying it. Don't start laughing. No, don't make me laugh. Oh, I remember how we used to lecture men on togetherness. D'you remember our 'joy and fulfilment of being *around* someone' speech? Oh, *don't*. I haven't laughed like this for ages. Hey, d'you remember 'your very own person'? I can't believe

Hemmed in by love

it. I mean that's all we ever wanted. Oh, don't. I'm only laughing this much because I'm tired. Oh, space. Didn't we say we'd swipe behind the knees the next man we met who talked about his *space*? I can't believe we're having this conversation. You and me wanting space. No, I *know* it's different. The men we knew used to want space so that they could meet other women. I mean don't we *know* it? Men are so funny about that aren't they? They seem to understand you might want to work. They *insist* on it. But they don't seem to take the rest of your life into account. They assume it will revolve around them. No, there's no one else I want to go out with either. He's my favourite man. I haven't a clue where we'd find men if we wanted them. Are you crazy? Don't you read the newspapers? There aren't any men about. It's been officially confirmed. They're married, gay, or certifiable. Single women over 30 are desperate and lonely. I keep reading it.

No, I know *we* weren't. But we were sort of wistful sometimes, weren't we? Yes, my mother keeps telling me I'm not getting any younger. I wasn't getting any younger at eight years old. Listen, Freud maintained that life was about Love and Work. We've got both those things. He didn't say space. Look, I know Freud is not around when you're going crazy trying to get ready for the office in the morning. I don't know why men keep looking at their watches when you're trying to find your bra and tights. They just *do*. Don't talk mornings, I start to go off men altogether. No, of course I'm not sleeping properly. Freud did not say Spending The Night Together and Work. You're absolutely right. Separate houses could be the answer. Oh... Don't yawn down the phone like that. It's catching. I don't know when I'll see *you* either. The next couple of weeks looks hopeless. Yes, I miss *you* enormously. This is like having a stolen chat with a lover. We really should try and see each other soon, even if there is no time. No, I never would have guessed it would be like this. Of *course* it'll work out. One way. Or the other.

Another night upon the tiles . . .

Sweet Dalmane and Mogadon,
where has all your magic gone?
Don't you know it's hard to be
this wide awake at 3.03?

Eight hours' sleep's a work girl's must,
and I've invested so much trust
in fifteen milligram Dalmane
how *could* you let me down again?

You work for three hours then down tools,
do sleeping pills have union rules?
Oh those long hours you used to keep.
Those blissful nights of eight hours' sleep.

This three-hour stint's a crazy joke.
I rise, I swear, drink tea and smoke,
reflect with grim nocturnal sorrow
how ravaged I will look 'tomorrow'.

How I will be teased and kidded
as I stumble heavy-lidded
to an office bright with smiles
'Another night upon the tiles?'

Insomniacs are much maligned,
and those who sleep can be unkind.
There should be some society
like the AA or RAC.

Another night upon the tiles . . .

When there's a breakdown in your slumber,
you dial a sleepless person's number.
Of course they can't *do* anything
but an a.m. shared is comforting.

But caution please in ringing me,
I'm comatose from 12 till 3.
I'm bushy tailed from 3 till 4,
but after that – I can't be sure.

At six if you've an urge to speak,
I'm willing but I'm awfully weak.
At 8 o'clock, well need I say,
I happily could sleep all day . . .

P'raps that's the answer, p'raps I should,
the daily sleep would do me good.
Dreamy days spent softly snoozing,
and night work might be quite amusing.

Bloody hell, it's gone 4 now,
I've got to get some sleep somehow.
A person hasn't any right
to *day* dream at this time of night.

Relax relentless writhing brain,
no, you can't have more Dalmane . . .
Amor is supposed to *vincit omnia*,
p'raps that's the cure for my insomnia.

Hello, I'm Desperate

*T*he phone rings and a female voice says, 'Hello, I'm Desperate.' There is no other introduction, no other name given. 'Desperate' is the caller's name. It has an urgent, racy, dramatic ring to it. I am responsive to drama. 'What *is* it?' I say. 'What's happened?'

'Oh *you* wouldn't understand,' says Desperate.

Try me. My level of comprehension has been raised no end these past couple of years. And I'm alert, responsive. I can move fast when the situation calls. Is the house on fire? Have you been attacked? Has the bank suddenly foreclosed on you? Are you pregnant? Has someone been *very* unkind? Why do you sound as if you're on the run? Tell me, tell me. I'll do anything I can to help ... I'm tensed in readiness....

'What can I do?' I say. '*Please* tell me what's the matter?'

There's a pause. And then, 'Well, I don't have a man and I'm sick to death of living like this. Sick to death of pretending things are OK.'

My shoulders droop with relief. My body goes from tensed to relaxed to floppy. It's someone else signing on to participate in the current 'I can't go on without a man' game that is becoming the new international rage for non-thinking women over the age of 25. Any two people can play this game. Player Number One is the person who 'can't go on', but she does for a minimum of 15 minutes' telephone time. She is the only person who has ever experienced Real Pain, Wretched Depression and Unbearable Loneliness. Player Number Two must possess no personal feelings, be prepared to accept certain unintentional insults, and should not contradict any statements of Player Number One. Otherwise it can turn ugly ... Player Number One calls or yelps *all* the shots which is

Hello, I'm Desperate

sometimes frustrating for Player Number Two but that is a firm rule of the game.

'That's hardly desperate. Lots of women don't have men. And loads of men don't have women.'

'You *don't* understand, do you? You haven't got a clue how I feel.'

No, of course I don't know. I am single, female and without a special man at the moment. But I have obviously been neutered. Unintentional insult. Point to First Player.

'I *do* understand that you're unhappy. Truly, I'm sorry. I hate you being miserable. It's just that I'm trying to tell you that lots of people don't have men. I can't see it as tragic or life threatening.' Another bad move. Player Number One gets snappy.

'That doesn't console me for a moment. I don't care about them. I care about *me*.' No kidding, Number One. You had me fooled there for a minute. I struggle back to the required pose and correct tone of a good Number Two. A sympathetic and optimistic move is now needed.

'Oh come on. Your life is very good. You like your job. Your flat is lovely. You've good friends. And there are lots of men out there who'd love to meet someone like you.'

Go back three spaces, Number Two. Will you never get the hang of this? Number One is now entitled to an Exasperated Big Yelp. 'I need a *special* man. Someone who will adore me and bloody well fall in love with me. I need a sex life with someone who's mad about me. I need a relationship. A normal life. I can't go on like this.'

A tricky moment. Number One is well in the lead and it's hard to figure what she really means. Is this a sign that a) she wants me to fix her up with a real, live, incredibly attractive man I'm not using at the moment? b) she is thinking of killing herself? c) she is livid at my simplistic view of this grave situation? 'Look. I do understand that it's nice to have someone around. Sometimes it's very nice – wonderful. But surely a man isn't the only thing in life?' Wrong, wrong, wrong Number Two. Really you're having an off day.

'Tell me something *better* than a man.' Ouch. There's real sarcastic triumph in the voice. I *defy* you to come up with something better. Top that you feminist bigshot. Go on, top 'a man'.

Hello, I'm Desperate

This calls for swift lateral thinking. I am having to defend my position as a single, contented manless person. And it's silly having to defend something you don't feel that aggressive about. Life is terrific with a man. Life can also be terrific without one special man. Men are great to spend time with, live with. They're not what you *do* in life. There's a whole world of things to do and people to meet. Is not Number One a little obsessed by this game? She knows that I think being in love is wonderful, but she also knows I love *living*. Try again.

'Look, it's not really a question of what's better than a man. I mean, compared to what? What about friends? Fun and company? Doing the things you've always said you want to do – like catching up on a few films, seeing your girlfriends, reading, going to the country for a weekend, trying to paint, write? What about spending time with you? Getting to know you. If you're relaxed in your *own* company and happy with youself, it's easier to be close to someone else one day. Men sense if you're 'needy' and they run a mile. I would.' Lose an immediate ten points for downright stupidity.

'I hate being alone. I loathe my own company. I want to share my life with someone. I don't want to do those things, anyway. I want a man to care for me and cherish me. I want to *share* things. What's wrong with that?'

The end of the game is in sight. Number Two, you're losing hands down as usual. Number One has obviously read *Why do I Think I'm Nothing Without a Man?* Or at least the title has firmly embedded itself in her consciousness and you can't win now. She's miles ahead with all her 'I wants'. She is purposefully vague here to force me into a no-points question. I give in. 'What kind of things do you want to share?' I say.

'Oh you know exactly what I mean. *Everything*.'

This reply temporarily beats the hell out of even the most experienced Number Two Players. Most Number One Players get up, go to work, tidy their flats (optional), go shopping, hit the occasional exercise class, buy clothes and cosmetics, read a bit, watch TV, phone their girlfriends and think about why they haven't got a man. What's to share with Number One? Her space? Her body? Her mind? Her food? Her deep need for someone of the opposite sex? She probably doesn't want to

Hello, I'm Desperate

share her income. She's making it very clear that she doesn't like her life at all. Why on earth would a person want to share something she can't stand with someone else? Hmm. Puzzling. Ah! Got it. It was simple, really.

'You mean you want to share someone *else's* life?' A definite three points for bull's eye accuracy and a further two if no offence is caused.

'Of *course* I do. It's only natural. It's all right for you, *you* can cope. But I need a man.'

Here, hang on Number One. I know it's utterly against the rules to tell you that I'm very fond of my life, but you can't be so lacking in perception that you think what I do is 'coping'. Look up 'coping' in the dictionary: I think it's what married women with four children and no help do. I must remember the game. Of course your mental, physical and emotional equipment is much more geared to a man than mine could ever be. I keep forgetting I'm meant to be neutered . . . Oh well, one last shot at getting you to be cheerful. Try the Helpful Constructive Suggestions Ploy. And keep your personal feelings out of it. This conversation is not about you, Number Two.

'Well if you hate being alone and feel you desperately need to meet a man then why don't you go out and mix more? You can go to dinner parties and cocktail parties. Or come to that, you could give them. You could invite all your single girlfriends and ask them to bring a man friend, someone they're not involved with, and then see who you like.

'You can go to gallery openings. There's always fascinating lectures on somewhere and people often have a drink afterwards. What about political meetings? At least you'll meet a man who's voting the same way. I'd answer one of those funny ads in the personal columns, or maybe I'd put one in myself. Or take up a sport – men love sports. The tennis club, what about that? You've always said you'd adore to be able to play a game of tennis. Men are found in tennis clubs, you know. I love evening classes – you learn something and you meet people. It's marvellous. Honestly, it isn't difficult to meet men. Half the population are men. And I should think they'd be thrilled to meet someone who shared the same interests, particularly if she's attractive.'

Number One comes up with her winning speech. 'Don't be so

Hello, I'm Desperate

ridiculous. Why on earth would an interesting man be doing any of those things? If a man is interesting he's *with* someone. He doesn't need to do all that rubbish. I mean, if a man is that desperate to meet someone, I certainly wouldn't want to meet him. God, no.'

Go and wash your mouth out with soap, Number Two, and never, ever tell Number One where you met all those delicious men you've known. It's obvious to any Number One player that they were out and about at dinners and *soirées* and evening classes and friends' houses and blind dates and down in the country and speaking to you over the white wine at the Folio Fine Art Society because they were desperate. No, they wouldn't be her type at all ... Sorry kid, you've just lost another game.

For Katharine

Though certain men had tendered bids
I'd never really thought of kids
My life lacked vital discipline
To fit a tiny baby in.
Then I saw Katie . . .

I'd put up that familiar fight.
'I'll do it when the timing's right'
Which is a silly thing to say
As I thought that September day
When I met Katie.

A five-pound wondrous happening
Delivered in the Lindo Wing,
St Mary's. The most perfect child.
They gave her to me and Kate smiled
When I held Katie.

There was an instant sweet rapport
formed in the Lindo corridor
between that new-born babe and me.
I loved her instantaneously
When I held Katie.

I talk as though she were my own
But darling Kate belongs to Joan
my special New York/London friend
with whom I stayed for months on end
Next door to Katie.

For Katharine

She's like a miniature Holbein
She hugs me and she feels like mine.
Oh sometimes feelings half-suppressed
well silently within my breast
When I hug Katie ...

I've so loved watching Katie grow
She's four years old this year you know
My life still lacks the discipline
To fit a tiny baby in
So I share Katie ...

Reflections on rejection

*T*here may be a foolproof way to handle rejection, but if there is I never got to hear about it. I've either been stunned with surprise or outraged at the awful timing. Once or twice I've been so paralysed with misery at the thought of going on without the other person that I didn't think I'd survive. It's funny how you do. You learn all sorts of things about yourself and your friends and very often the man in question. Sometimes, as Scott Fitzgerald said, 'You become a different person and the different person wants different things.'

In retrospect the situations in my life have been ludicrous, a relief, the wrong person at the right time (and vice versa), part of the sadistic game-play of a long love affair or merely a man being practical. At the time, of course, it was hell. When those memorable clichés: 'This relationship isn't going anywhere', 'Let's not see each other for a while', 'I don't think I'm ready for commitment' and 'There doesn't seem much point in this' hit the air, I crumble. My heart slithers down into some unknown medical region in my stomach while my mind insists that this isn't happening to me. Once, in Jamaica, I got the distinct impression that I was being machine-gunned in slow-motion. When the man has really mattered I've refused to accept rejection and I've stayed around gamely like a staggering punch-drunk fighter. Or like a masochist, as a psychiatrist pointed out. But I always believed in seeing something through to the end and not just leaving because a man *said* it was the end in mid-affair.

Of course, you do have to understand yourself and your *real* feelings and the man and his real depth of emotions. Easier said than done. But twice in my life I've suspected that the men who said goodbye weren't

Reflections on rejection

ready to go or to have me leave. And so more or less I stayed. Maybe I thought love was too precious, too rare to walk out on with my pride intact. And so I didn't.

Listen, I don't know that I recommend it to the over-sensitive or uncertain. You can go through even more agony to find out that your refusal to accept an ending was, after all, a dreadful mistake and the man really *had* changed his mind about you. There is always Oscar Wilde's nagging thought, 'There's nothing more ridiculous than the passions of one whom one has ceased to love'.

Obviously it depends who is rejecting you and why. Sometimes it helps to understand the reason. I mean there's always room for self-improvement. Of course men don't always feel they have to spell it out and sometimes there is nothing to say. It could be that their curiosity – often sexual – was satisfied after a few dates. This does feel like blunt rejection and it hurts. But the truth is you weren't really accepted in the first place. This hindsight admittedly doesn't help when you're in a state of high excitement and have tumbled into bed with him fantasising about a holiday together or wondering what it would be like to live with him. It's as well not to confuse sex with being cared about. Oh, I've heard men say, 'I *never* sleep with people I don't *like*' but I've noticed that their 'fondness' for women often doesn't manifest itself outside the bedroom.

What is true is that a man who rejects you often becomes enormously attractive to you while you feel like a creeping failure. You aren't worth his time, therefore it follows you must be worthless. I've lost vital parts of my equipment at such times: my confidence, my sense of humour, my interest in anyone else, any hope for the future and the ability to string together a sentence without the mention of *his* name. I didn't know that local geography could be so painful. The Bayswater Road, King's Road, Fulham Road, Mount Street and whole sections of SW1, SW7, Battersea and Holland Park have all been no-go areas in their time.

It's a maddening quirk of human nature that what you *can't* have often becomes very desirable. Similarly, people are convinced that if they pay a high price for something, then it must be worth having. I've only to look in my wardrobe to know the fallacy of *that*

Reflections on rejection

statement. One of the men I cared about, who is now a good friend and still a rejector of unsurpassed calibre, said only recently that rejection is a great aphrodisiac. He could have mentioned this earlier in our relationship I think. I spent years finding him irresistible and wasted dozens of chicken-wish bones saying, 'Please let him love me'.

If I'm honest I understand in each and every case why I was 'rejected'. Well I know now. I *can't* pretend I was filled with understanding those weekends when I huddled on the sofa in a small ball of misery while Paul Williams' reedy voice moaned for me. 'Loneliness makes the winter nights seem far too long, makes the summer sunshine much too strong.' Dammit, why did I *put* myself through that? There were also the soggy toast and mugs of warm tea days to the strains of, 'They're writing songs of love but not for me'. It's a marvellous song, by the way, and it only hurts if you want it to. No, I *didn't* understand as I stared at the skies through the windows of the flat that was so special that, 'You'll never be depressed here'. Who *said* that? They should be strung up.

Oddly enough I used to have rules about rejection. I always told myself, and anyone who'd listen, that I'd accept defeat gracefully if I'd been rejected for a superior. My loved one could leave with my tearful blessing if he produced a combination of Christie Brinkley, Simone de Beauvoir and Barbra Streisand. I mean, fair's fair, *I'd* leave me. Come to think of it, I might have rejected everybody except perhaps one man, and I can't swear to it if Woody Allen had been knocking my door down. But he wasn't and so I've had to struggle by as best I could. I have been temporarily or permanently passed over in favour of an ex-wife, a three-year-old daughter, a career, a stunning older woman, his mother, one of my girlfriends, Miss World and a man. And, I suppose, I should add that there were a couple of men who talked about space when it was fashionable and one man who said 'I want to be alone' in a tone of voice that made Greta Garbo sound gregarious. I remember some of the parting conversations:

'What can you see in a 20-year-old who's Miss World?'
'That's right. That's exactly what I see in her.'
'Why didn't you tell me your ex-wife is living with you?'
'She's not *living* with me. She's just moved back, that's all.'

Reflections on rejection

'What do you mean you've been seeing a lot of my friend Katy?'

'I mean I've been seeing all of her.'

'Oh, for goodness' sake Marce, why do you have to take my having an affair as a rejection of *you*. Why can't you see it as my acceptance of someone else?'

'You could have mentioned *en passant* that you were having an affair with a man.'

'My private life is my own business.'

You know it has occurred to me that men think differently ... But everyone is entitled to change their mind. If no one had any second thoughts about anyone we'd all be ambling on until death with our very first dates. Someone has to do some rejecting. Those of us who are single have to understand that it's a free market.

Yes, I *know* married people change their minds and shop around, but that's another article. You and the men you know are entitled to shop around for what you want. As you know, people shop differently. Some have very fixed ideas about what they're looking for, and while they may dally momentarily over something else that catches their eye, they often remain single-minded in their initial objective. Some people will buy *anything*. Then there are those who dismiss something good on the grounds that it's too readily available. Some people are so drunk with their spending power they don't value things. Others are too mean to buy anything. Some wise and lucky people recognise something of terrific value and snap it up. And some people when they've found exactly what suits them then decide they can't afford it

I get *exhausted* just thinking about the whole selection and rejection process. Currently I'm not shopping – I'm using the men I've acquired over the years. But to be honest, stocks are running low and I may have to leap out into the market place one day quite soon. If you're suffering rejection, you have my tremendous sympathy. You're probably a bargain. Lots of us are.

There's an upmarket reject shop in Knightsbridge, near where I live. I should check it out one of these weekends. Maybe I'll see you in there.

When oft upon my couch
I lie . . .

*N*ow I don't feel any pain
I should consider love again
and not let months and years roll by
at least I ought to have a try.

Its all too easy on one's own
supportive friends – a telephone
and of course I have to mention
the marked absence of love's tension.

But memories and sentiment
mean I dwell on what it meant
to love another loving soul
life was sweeter, I felt whole.

I slump and gaze with dreamy stares
remembering my love affairs
my mind is cute and must be credited
all the bitter bits get edited.

Mmm – some warm man to court me, bait me
someone smart to motivate me
be romantic, sentimental
intelligent but not judgemental.

When oft upon my couch I lie ...

Give me space, be unsuspicious
always find me quite delicious
he'll love my body and my brain
and I'll be great in bed again....

I know I cannot lift a finger
to find a love song or a singer
if *you* could send a man along
well who knows – I might try a song.

But now I have no energy
so brave new man must come to me
it is chutzpah I confess –
could *you* give him my home address.

Head Start

My erogenous zone
is so sadly unknown
to the average man that I see
he will subtly grope
stiff with sexual hope
that he'll get the same rise out of me

I am *not* thrilled to bits
as his hands cup my tits
it's then that he faces rejection
dammit why can't he see
that a 'she's' like a 'he'
but I need a mental erection

Could a man not aspire
to aim somewhat higher
than breasts and vagina terrain
it's the way I'm designed
can't he massage my mind?
could he start his foreplay with my brain?

If bodies they fancy
then why can't a man see
the way to my body pale brown
is cerebral stroking
I *swear* I'm not joking
Lover – start with my *head* and work down

Hurrah for the holiday harlot

*T*ake a nice British girl, remove outer clothing, place on foreign beach at 80° F and wait until lightly brown. Add a man and stand clear, then watch her *sizzle*. And possibly even scorch her way into the newspapers. 'Topless Tina makes love on Greek beach'; 'Naked romp amazes locals'; 'Briton in nude orgy rumpus'. Yes, it's us. At it again. Being *scandalous* on our holidays. What on earth gets into us? No, I don't want your answers on a postcard. But you've got to admit that, if the press are to be believed, we do have a reputation for outrageous behaviour when we're far away from home. Yes, I *know* the Swedes and Germans do it. Not to mention the Finns. But they do it at home. We don't.

Sometimes I've read lurid accounts of holiday 'scandals' when I've been on holiday. The odd thing is, when I'm stretched out on some foreign beach, tanned, topless and tipsy, the stories don't seem outrageous at all. They're a sort of dizzy extension of what I'm doing myself. Or thinking about. Words like 'naked' and 'nude' or even 'orgy' have little shock value when you're wearing almost nothing and you're aware that the nice, giggly crowd from Guildford had what freckly Sharon described as 'an incredibly funny party' in one of the rooms last night. So the party got a bit out of hand and there were a few complaints. But looking at Sharon laughing with her new friends the morning after – well, it hardly seems a scandal. They look as if they're having fun. Gosh, I don't mind if they do.

Ah. But I do grant you that when I read the same stories in London

Hurrah for the holiday harlot

W11 on one of those workaday August mornings then I am truly shocked. It's incredible to read of such wanton behaviour when I'm clutching a mug of tea, dicing with the idea of taking off my thermal vest and wondering why I can't even get a builder, let alone a lover. Nude orgies? Who *are* these people? Tourists to this country don't behave like that – as the press points out. In fact, nobody behaves like that here which is presumably one of the reasons we have to get away from it all. You could say that the atmosphere is compellingly non-conducive to larky behaviour. I think it's perfectly obvious why foreign tourists to Britain in the 18–30 age group do not run naked and drunk down the corridors in *our* hotels. They probably can't get a drink when they want one and they don't feel like jettisoning their clothes, given our social and meteorological conditions. They don't come here for that sort of fun. But they like us because we are polite, reserved, calm, conservative. 'Britain is such a *civilised* society,' they say with respect. Well, for civilised read repressed. We repress our emotions, our sexuality and our aggressions. I tell you, being civilised takes a lot out of you. If you still have a sexual flame, you're forced to keep it burning low. Yes, mine's gone out too. I'm trying not to dwell on it. But, as you well know, torrid does not get standing ovations in London and the Home Counties and it's positively frowned on in Birmingham and Liverpool. It seems we've actually cornered the world market in bottling it up. And so for 50 weeks of the year that's how we live. Properly and demurely.

It's not difficult in a country where most men place a love life 74th on the list of things they'd most like. Oh, Englishmen *can* be pleasant and I'm sure it would be possible to work up an appetite for them if *only* they'd get steamed up about us. But they don't and the signs are not encouraging. Englishmen are traditionally embarrassed by sex, puzzled by women and horrified by displays of passion. They like their women passive. Look, they don't *mind* a naked woman as long as it's not you and as long as they're not actually called upon to get *involved* with her. I mean, they'll happily mob a supermarket because Maria Whittaker will be there 'in the flesh' as the newspapers hint provocatively. But what's good about Maria is she doesn't actually *do* anything except smile and show her tits on page three. A passionate woman is not necessarily

Hurrah for the holiday harlot

regarded as a domestic or social asset and Englishmen do not allot much time to private pleasure. God, it's no wonder that we women are apt to pop our corks when we reach those sun-drenched enthusiastic foreign islands where the men are *thrilled* to see us.

Have you noticed, by the way, that it is so much easier to shed your clothes and inhibitions where English isn't spoken? It's part of the collective British fantasy that sexual frolics won't be understood in a different language. We tend to be more self-conscious if the natives speak our mother tongue, which could be why we're less frisky in the USA or Caribbean. The holiday scandals invariably come from Greece, Spain and Italy and mostly they're about sex and always about women. English *men* don't rate as many column inches in the newspapers unless they're at it with us. As far as our men are concerned, mostly it's the 'Drunken spree lands Brits in jail' stuff that hits the headlines as they thrill to the heady delights of round-the-clock alcohol, knocking over chairs and each other in seaside restaurants, and pushing passing people into swimming pools. Oh well. Boys will be boisterous. It's scandalous that that is all they can think of doing.

But it's not what we want to read about, is it? And the newsmen know it. Can you *imagine* the lives of the frazzled features editors of *The Sun*, the *Daily Mirror* and the *News of the World*, sitting in stuffy, overcrowded Fleet Street offices with the phones ringing non-stop? They can't get a drink when they want one – always – and summer is trickling by outside. Suddenly, up on the wires comes a report of British girls being arrested for romping around with no clothes on or indulging in wild lovemaking with some bloody foreigner in the Greek heat of the midday sun. You bet a features editor recognises a scorching scandal. Dammit, he's outraged. He can't get booze and sex when he wants it. He's working.

It's all too much for him. He writes out his frustrations in lines of steamy copy, knowing that the rest of us in repressed Britain will be provoked, shocked and very titillated. We're all fascinated to read about *anyone* having sex – particularly one of us. It *does* show that given the right circumstances it can be done. Of course, male readers are equally stirred. 'Why does that sort of thing never happen to me?' asked my nice

Hurrah for the holiday harlot

insurance man. 'You'd never get that in Romford.' Thousands of readers are predictably offended by such shenanigans and thousands more experience *frissons* of excitement when they realise their own holidays are but weeks away. But I want to ask you something. Could it be that, with a few exceptions, and with the drunken sprees apart, only the *British* are scandalised by the way that some British holidaymakers behave abroad? The French are not moved to comment about frolicking sex and nudity at their seaside resorts – unless the people concerned are well known. Heavens, no – the French invented all that. And the Italians, Greeks and Spanish, passionate people themselves, seem to have come to terms with the fact that (a) their summer days are hot and (b) the tourists might well act oddly once they have taken off most of their clothes.

And equally they're not given to writing about the 'scandalous' carryings-on of young tourists. Partly they *expect* all tourists to behave badly and partly they're not at all surprised that foreign women take a sexual shine to their handsome men. It all seems perfectly natural to them. They take it with a pinch of bottom. Do you suppose that despite our much aired indignation we have a sneaking fondness for our peculiarly British idea of holiday scandal? Making love or taking off all your clothes isn't really *hostile*, is it? You may think it rude, naughty or outrageous, but you've got to admit that nobody is actually *suffering*, are they? It's not as though we're shoplifting in foreign chain store equivalents of Marks & Spencer, having shoot-outs on foreign streets or littering foreign cities with illegally parked cars. At least, not often. Truth is, UK girls just wanna have fun. For two sweet, hot weeks we like to abandon ourselves to pleasure. And the rest of the summer months? We'll pull on our thermal vests, stock up on tea bags and tut tut at the newspaper reports along with the rest of the nation.

The going off of Mrs Roffe

Jackie's blonde, a warm delight,
the glitter girl who's up all night,
dressed in fashion's latest craze,
shopping wildly through the days.

Costly shoes on dainty feet
trip daily down South Molton Street
on missions purposeful and grave,
she's fashion's darling, fashion's slave.

Her not infrequent ups and downs
are cured by Saint Laurent and Browns.
She spends with ease, a lavish rogue,
on 'musts' in *Harpers, Elle* and *Vogue*.

I've made her seem banal and trite
which isn't fair and isn't right.
She's funny, bright, a marvellous friend
and honest to the bitter end.

The end came just the other day,
my phone rang, I heard Jackie say,
'Fashion does play dirty tricks,
its hellish being thirty-six.'

'My skin's okay, my figure's neat,
I didn't contract cellulite,
but *Vogue has* hit me where it hurts
page 163 shows mini-skirts ...'

114

The going off of Mrs Roffe

'Jack,' I giggled, 'let it go,
we socked it to 'em years ago.'
I heard a gentle Jackie groan
as she confided down the phone.

'I've been to Harrods, tried some on,
my *raison d'être's* vanished, gone
I'm really old, my life has stopped,
goddamit Marce, my knees have dropped.'

Footnote

I hope to God I never meet
a man who's deeply into feet.
They are my most unfavourite part
and I become most sick at heart
when threatened with the perfect man
whose sexual embracings can
discover each square inch of me.
I lie and pray that he won't see
those toes now permanently curled ...
I have the worst feet in the world.

I drape my body 'cross a sheet
and *pray* the covers hide my feet,
I writhe in each seductive pose
as long as he can't see my toes
and wildly lustful moments freeze
when love play's creeping past my knees.
(The sympathy I always feel
for poor Achilles and his heel.)
Erotic love was never born
amidst a bent toe and a corn.

Footnote

I vainly thought I could enlist
the help of a chiropodist.
He stared and coughed and cleared his throat
and asked me if I'd like 'a quote'.
'Of course, you could try Harley Street,
some surgeons specialise in feet.'
I bolted from his surgery
as fast as feet would carry me.
My lovers will be spared such shocks
in future I'll get laid in socks.

and Me

I'm a monkey junkie

*H*e was a soft greyish brown colour with anxious eyes and he needed a home. And I said could I hold him and picked him up and he clung to me. Two baby monkey arms were thrown about my neck and his small head buried itself in my collar. His body quivered and I'm afraid it was instant love. I said I wanted him and I'd learn how to feed him and look after him.

A week later, when I collected him, he seemed to be more cuddly and furry and bewildered than ever. He was wearing a loose collar around his tiny abdomen and he had a chain attached to the collar. 'Does he have to wear that?' I asked as my baby monkey pulled crossly at the red leather strap. 'I'm afraid he does when he's out of doors,' said the pet shop owner. 'If you let him off a lead he'll go away and never come back.' 'Sorry baby,' I whispered to the wriggling ball in my arms. 'It's only for now.' And I promised that things would get better.

The two of us climbed into a car that a friend of mine was driving. I fastened the monkey's chain to a long Victorian chain I was wearing over a baggy sweater. The little monkey, after a quick horrified look at the steering wheel, the view through the windscreen, my impatient friend and a passing lorry, made an instant decision. He pulled up my sweater and flung himself under it. For the remainder of the ride home he lay motionless with his arms stretching towards my waist and I could feel tiny fingers on my skin. He was so small you couldn't really see him from outside my sweater. Only I could feel a little heart beating. 'He thinks you're his mother,' said the man in the car and I said, 'Oh God, I think he's going to become a complete addiction.' By the time we'd arrived home I'd decided to call him Hash.

He wasn't at all interested in his new home. Not at all. What he most

I'm a monkey junkie

wanted to do was cling to me. I tried to talk him out of it which was silly as I thought later that it was probably Hash's way of bonding.

I didn't mean to introduce him to restaurant life so early on, and certainly the retaurant manager would have been horrified if he'd known that underneath my sweater was a baby java monkey. But Hash wouldn't come out from under and I figured nobody would notice, and that first day of our lives together Hash and I and three people I knew and four I didn't sat down for a hearty Saturday lunch. Hash had eaten breakfast and I'd been warned to feed him only twice a day or the consequences would be on my head. Or the carpet or wherever else Hash chose to relieve himself. The meal was boisterous, the friends were giggly, a visiting American was drinking too much and Hash seemed to be sleeping peacefully under my sweater. Everything was fine until the fourth or fifth bottle of red wine. The American had reached the drunken stage and insisted on more crudités even though most of us were just about to order coffee. The crudités came and were placed in front of me. Then it happened. Hash made a startling split-second appearance, grabbed a raw carrot and went straight back under my sweater. I remember biting my lip and waiting for the big eviction scene. But nobody had seen. No one in the entire restaurant had noticed. Except the American. He shook his head and put his glass down very slowly. 'I've had too much to drink,' he said to the woman next to him. 'I've definitely had too much to drink.' I could feel baby Hash munching at the carrot and I smiled at the American in the way you do when you want tourists to feel welcome.

That evening Hash came out. And his next social occasion was also a great success. He sat happily on my lap pulling at my chains while we ate dinner in a friend's flat at a big wooden table. He hopped onto the table, still attached to me, and approached a wine glass. Suddenly, he stood up, a big nine-inch monkey now, and he dipped one of his hands into the wine glass and scooped up a handful of claret. I was sure that wasn't on his recommended diet. But little eyes wrinkled with pleasure and little monkey lips were licked. He settled back on my lap with his arm thrown across me and he looked like a tired, contented little old man.

He slept that night chained to a big wooden box with a small blanket

121

I'm a monkey junkie

inside. But the next step would be a cage. A friend of mine volunteered to build it. There was just the question of where to put it. I suggested my bedroom which was quite large and airy besides which there wasn't really another room. It seems absurd now, but it didn't then. And so half my bedroom from ceiling to floor became a monkey house. Hash rather liked it. There were mirrors and toys and places for him to swing on, and there was a box for him to hide in or sulk in or think his private thoughts. My mother and other people said it was an awful way to live and what did I think I was doing. 'Wait till you see him,' I said.

Baby Hash was thriving and I changed my whole diet because of him. He adored fresh fruit and vegetables and he was a very fastidious eater. He'd peel everything very carefully. Nobody ever ate a grape with such finesse. I had half solved the problem of potty training, but there were still slight mishaps. After feeding him in the morning and evening I'd hold him over the lavatory and squeeze his tummy and wait. He wasn't fond of nappies although I tried. I tried washing him, too, but he wriggled incredibly and tried to bite me. But I knew there had to be a way around keeping him clean. Hash was totally contented provided he could follow me everywhere around the flat and this included the bathroom. One day I was lying in the bath with him watching me from the handbasin and playing with the soap. He was by now very frisky and confident, although his baby leaps often ended with him crashing on the floor. This day as I smiled at him he decided to leap. He landed in the bath and I screamed. Just as I leapt out wondering what on earth you do to revive a drowning monkey, I saw that he was doing an extraordinary monkey paddle in the warm water. 'Hash!' I yelled. 'You can *swim*.' And I fished him out as he neared the bath taps. A small dripping rat of a person with teeth chattering and what I swear was a smile on his face. He loathed and resented being dried in the big bath towel and bared his teeth at me. But he didn't at all mind the Johnson's baby powder being rubbed into his little tummy. And so we solved the cleaning problem.

I often took Hash out with me, but even though he was the most special and affectionate monkey, I can't say we were welcome everywhere. He would still cling happily inside a sweater, but these days his small head would bob up over the top and best of all he liked sitting

I'm a monkey junkie

on my shoulder. He loved walks in the park and visits to antique shops and he adored the car. Best of all he liked to sit and stare out of the window behind the back seat but he was a kind of road hazard. Every time we stopped at the lights he'd leap from the back seat to my shoulder and it had a bad effect on the drivers around me. Once I took him to a live TV show. He stayed inside my sweater but this time he wasn't fastened as securely as usual and he escaped halfway through the programme. I am never, ever allowed back in BBC Television Centre, Shepherd's Bush as long as I live.

Little Hash had a way of reflecting my every mood. When I was happy and dancing around the flat, he would dance with me. When I was at my most affectionate, Hash would play with me for ages and groom my hair so carefully. Best of all he loved my elbows. He'd pull on the loose skin and make funny little kissing noises with his puckered mouth. I made them back, of course.

He was an integral part of my life and even my family had met him. My grandmother loved him and my mother grudgingly admitted that he was OK but said wasn't he a substitute for something else? That was rather a gut-crunching remark I thought as I watched my brothers rolling with him on the floor. 'I do love you so much, baby Hash' I told him as we drove back from Leigh-on-Sea.

The crunch came a couple of months later when I had to move into a new flat and there were positively, absolutely and definitely no pets allowed. I thought it was a thudding omen. Hash was bigger and stronger now and even though he adored me and preferred me to anybody, he didn't mind at all being with other people. Of course I didn't ask him what he really felt because I didn't want to hear the answer. I spent one utterly sad weekend in the flat we'd both soon have to leave. I couldn't face seeing or speaking to anyone. Most of the weekend I sat dully in an armchair contemplating a Hashless future. Tears came and went and came again. Silent, aching stuff. And Hash was so quiet and sweet and dreadfully loving. He didn't once leave me and he slept in my bed with his arms curled around my head.

The following week I put an ad in *The Times* personal column. 'Adorable baby monkey, tame and affectionate, seeks loving home.'

I'm a monkey junkie

The phone rang constantly with people from all over Britain who wanted Hash. One duchess, five writers, four country doctors, umpteen people who just said they'd always wanted a monkey and one man called Don who was the first to call and rang me every hour. I took a few phone numbers and rushed home at the end of the day to hug Hash. I crept into his cage and held him to me and rocked back and forth and tried hard not to cry.

I dialled Don's number. 'Could I just ask you about yourself?' I said. Don told me he shared a flat with Althea, a wonderful woman who was mad about monkeys. 'We'll give him the most marvellous life,' he said. 'And as we're practically neighbours, you can visit him whenever you want. You know, like a divorced person who has constant access to the child.'

I knew that life would never be the same again without him, and it wasn't. Order and relative sanity returned to my flat and I went on a very regular basis to Don and Althea's luxury penthouse around the corner. Hash was almost hysterically pleased to see me at first and I soon stopped feeling tearful every time I had to leave. He was living so well and was obviously thrilled with his ritzy new surroundings. Althea used to hug me and say, 'You've no idea how much we love him' and I have to admit it made me feel good to realise he'd grown up to be such a nice person.

I still miss his funny monkey smell and no one else has ever hugged me in quite the same way. Dogs and cats are, well, OK. But once you've had a real give and take relationship with a monkey nothing else will do. I never buy grapes without thinking of him, I never look at the monkeys in Regent's Park Zoo without yearning for him.

When oft upon my couch I lie thinking about those I have loved, I realise that Hash was indeed one of the loves of my life.

Cynics

*G*enerally cynics are not popular.
People don't like to see them or be them,
because cynics see things just the way that they are
not the way that you'd like them to see them.

Tough and tender views of Christmas

*L*ook, it's not that I don't love London or England. England is *brilliant* at some things like spring and autumn and, yes, I love crisp winter and even those thoughtful leaden skies and June is practically perfect. But *Christmas*? Oh my God. England assumes that everyone will be making their own merry little arrangements and London moodily shuts down for the best part of the worst two weeks of the year. I mentally go into sharp decline which in truth I've been doing ever since Father Christmas stopped dropping by at my place.

People I know flee from the city as if it had been designated a major plague area. They fling themselves into cars, trains, buses, planes – anything, just to get out of town. 'We're off to Scotland'; 'There's a family get-together in Newcastle'; 'I'm going *home* for Christmas'. If home is where the heart is, then few people seem to have a home in London. Do people just work here?

I used to wander disconsolately to Leigh-on-Sea and climb out at a railway station which hasn't changed in 30 years. A brother or two would pick me up and we'd hug each other. My mother would say sorry there's nothing to do down here but it's lovely to see you all anyway. My father who left home years ago but sometimes comes back for Sunday lunch was usually there on Christmas Day. It was friendly, affectionate stuff, but we were all agreed once my brothers got into their teens that you couldn't really stretch it out. I'd get back to London a couple of days later and see other dulled friends who'd been 'home for Christmas'.

Tough and tender views of Christmas

Everyone said, 'Phew, it's nearly over', as if Christmas was some kind of awful endurance test. I kept thinking there's got to be something better than this.

Once Selwyn and I got the Christmas dreads simultaneously when he was getting divorced and I was having one of those love affairs where a man suddenly starts to wrap important looking presents for his ex-wife and small daughter. 'I have to spend Christmas with them,' he said. 'You do understand, don't you?' 'Of *course*,' I said. 'We single childless people know that Christmas is *only* for families.'

Selwyn said that all things being considered our situations called for drastic action and we'd better get as far away as possible. And so we scampered off to Heathrow Airport on 19th December and boarded a plane for Mombasa. No, of course I couldn't afford it. But financially and emotionally I've never been good at budgeting.

The days before Christmas passed in a haze of African sun and baking white sand and tall elegant blacks with sinewy limbs who strolled along the beaches and sometimes came to talk to us. Selwyn had brought his drawing pad and sketched while I read and we'd sit in the shade of the palm trees bent low by the African winds. We explored Mombasa town and got to know a Masai tribesman who invited us to his village in a clearing in the jungly undergrowth. And as we sipped tea surrounded by our Masai's extended family, Selwyn said it's funny but you really could get away from it all if you tried. That night was Christmas Eve and as we sat on the terrace planning our safari to Treetops and Masai Mara, Selwyn leaned across and said, 'Guess who's coming for dinner.'

I shan't forget my sight of 12 black children in white angel frocks pulling a sleigh on which sat Father Christmas surrounded by sacks of presents. I said I thought I was going to cry. Father Christmas gave children of all ages a present and a middle-aged German on the next table almost threw down his champagne in the excitement of meeting a chuckling black Santa Claus and receiving a gift. '*Ich habe ein elephant,*' he yelled with the general sophistication of a thrilled five-year-old. Selwyn got a small wooden giraffe and I still have my carved rhinoceros. While the garden full of people were still oohing and aahing over their toys, Father Christmas started singing *Silent Night* in his low, round,

Tough and tender views of Christmas

rich voice. And as all the people joined in the singing, voices in different languages trilled across the warm air. All was calm. All was bright.

During that incredible week on safari we forgot everything and everybody. It was a shock to land in London in early January but we were so shot full of intense Kenyan memories that a deep contentment stayed with us for weeks.

Then there was the time Annette said, 'We've got to do *something* about bloody Christmas. What about a health farm?' And so we hit the road to Champneys. They don't have surprise Father Christmases or holly or a single silver bauble in sight. But they do have wonderful masseurs to soothe away a year's tension and it's surprising how much you get to like the green and white Light Diet Room, to say nothing of the wonderment you feel as you watch inches melt off your thighs after your daily dose of Slendertone.

We exercised a bit and read masses and caught up on sleep we'd missed out on for at least 10 years. I thought Annette was terribly clever to think of a health farm. By New Year's Eve when people were saying to me I looked absolutely marvellous and where had I *been* I thought she was probably a genius.

One year I ran to Jamaica to meet H which was nearly unfortunate as I got out of the plane at Montego Bay and he was waiting for me at Kingston. Most of Christmas Day was spent in a clattering taxi across rough roads in a monsoon trying to get to him. That was expensive. And frankly it wasn't our best holiday. The beginning of the end, as I remember. And once I liked Antigua and a house on Mill Reef called 'Turquoise' but that's when love and Christmas seemed to magically coincide. You can't normally plan that.

But I have to tell you that my absolutely favourite Christmas place is New York. As you cross the Triboro bridge on your way into Manhattan and you see that fantastic, jagged man-made skyline twinkling against the sky, you feel you're going to the very heart of the world. Whenever I get my first view of the city I need to catch my breath. It never fails to thrill me. Miraculously now, because of friends and memories and because the city is so welcoming, it feels like home.

And I've discovered over the years that despite my avowed anti-

Tough and tender views of Christmas

Christmas stance I really do feel like being sentimental and celebrating. But I need to be somewhere that's tremendously enthusiastic about Christmas. I need a place that loves itself and everyone else loves. People don't *leave* New York at Christmas. They *flock* to it. The roads and train stations and airports are crowded with people who can't wait to *get* to New York. Once I was standing at Kennedy Airport next to a pin-striped man with first class stickers on his luggage. He was softly singing, 'New York, New York, it's a wonderful town' as he piled his cases on to his trolley.

You should see Park Avenue in December. From 90th Street all the way down to Grand Central Station they plant Christmas trees and decorate them with shining white lights. Fifth Avenue, where the shops truly are the ritziest and glitziest and most exciting in the world, is a frenzied, people-packed spectacle with yellow cabs bumper to bumper. And there's the noise of their impatient horns as drivers lean out of windows to yell at other cars and pedestrians and there are the cries from the sidewalk vendors and the men roasting chestnuts and umpteen Father Christmases ringing their bells. And as Tiffany's, Bergdorf Goodman, Macy's, and thousands of other stores just *automatically* say 'Would you like this gift-wrapped?', people clutching their Christmas parcels look so, well, festive. Overhead, Christmas lights glitter as far as you can see.

Christmas shopping isn't the same in London – I don't have time to meet friends during the week and I *never* get dressed up for the sheer thrill of it. But in New York by mid-December I want to be as glossy and gleaming as the city itself. I want to jostle with those unashamedly glamorous New York women who rush out of Saks with their fur coats flying. And I do. And I love it. New Yorkers *use* their city and they're not at all intimidated by the ritziest places. 'Well, let's meet for tea at the Plaza,' they say. And you can sit amidst the pomp and the Palm Court orchestra and request Cole Porter tunes from a sweet piano. It doesn't cost anything except the price of a tea to watch the expensive world go by.

I have Christmas Eve memories of dinner with Marta at her house in Chelsea. She'd cooked three large geese and invited thirty of us to

Tough and tender views of Christmas

celebrate. At half past ten I left the party with Tom and we rushed to meet Erich outside St. Thomas's, the Episcopalian church on Fifth Avenue. There was a light mist hanging over the city and the cars were barely moving. There were thousands of pedestrians just strolling along, some with children, some with even smaller children in pushchairs. The air was warm and the atmosphere extraordinary. Gentle, sentimental, exciting. Like that old Hollywood movie, *Miracle on 34th Street*. The city seemed to acknowledge the special time and the feeling of togetherness.

When we got inside St. Thomas's I was stunned by the scene. 'Better than a Broadway show,' said Erich. 'Now you know why I had so much trouble reserving seats.' The altar was ablaze with candles, there were flowers everywhere, trails of green leaves wound around the pillars and choirboys in scarlet and white. I never sang *Hark, The Herald Angels Sing* with such gusto. When we left church, thousands of car horns were honking, but this time as apart of the celebration. Everyone was yelling 'Happy Christmas'.

I remember going to the theatre with Bonnie on Christmas Eve when the temperature was 21 degrees. And afterwards she said, 'It's great to walk through the city now' and we brisked our way to Rockefeller Plaza, too late to see the skaters on the ice rink, but time enough to stand with the crowds and join the carol singing. Sometimes New York is so sentimental it will even snow for you. And Manhattan under a light fall of snow on Christmas Eve with all lights shining from the tall buildings is one of the most beautiful sights imaginable.

Perhaps best of all, however tough and selfish the city appears to be, it really cares at Christmas. The TV, the newspapers, the stores and the offices never let you forget you're a privileged person (if you are). People in big corporations like IBM give up their Christmas Days to entertain the homeless and cook for them. One large company opens its entire building on Christmas Day so that old people can come and telephone their relatives all over the USA or everywhere in the world. The staff give up their day and man the telephone lines. The Sheraton Hotel gives a buffet lunch for 300 people who otherwise wouldn't be eating Christmas dinner. Macy's toy department is closed to the public one

Tough and tender views of Christmas

afternoon and opened to a large orphanage. The children are entertained and everyone gets a present. *The New York Times*, amidst its lavish Christmas advertisements, runs its own ads. They say, 'Remember the neediest.'

This Christmas I may be in England for the first time in years. I don't know how I feel about that but doubtless I'll survive it. But I do like knowing that *somewhere* in the world there are cities celebrating with zest, enthusiasm and caring. What my Christmas travels have shown me, apart from anything else, is that there *is* a Father Christmas. That's pretty good to know after years of disbelief. The thought will console me in Leigh-on-Sea, I think.

New York invite

I snuggled back in mellow mood
and filled with friendship, wine and food
I sat and gazed across the park
where New York glistens after dark
delighting in the City scene
the lights from 'Tavern on the Green'
I softened at my precious view
of wondrous Fifth Avenue.

Disturbing my sweet reverie
Joan handed me my English tea
She raised a welcoming eyebrow
'Please treat this place as home from now
don't feel you're just another guest'
How kind the sentiment expressed
I gazed amazed at Joan's calm face
Does she know how I treat my place?

If I imported home behaviour
I'd try the patience of a saviour
There's clutter reaching to my knees
I daily lose my front door keys
I wander 'round with nothing on
and wonder where my keys have gone
I drink a hundred cups of tea
The telephone rings constantly.

New York invite

Although these days I can afford a
cleaner, I'm a dreadful horder
She throws 'things' out and I'm bereft
(I raid the garbage when she's left)
My favourite lover does the cooking
which means the kitchen's ravaged looking
My friends call at 'unsocial' hours
I talk aloud to plants and flowers.

The bath has overflowed three times
while I was busy scribbling rhymes
the ceiling of the floor below
collapsed at the third overflow
anticipating what was coming
I blamed it on the lousy plumbing,
But gone was neighbourly endurance
He's claiming now from my insurance.

I think I'll break the news to Joan
I *daren't* treat her home as my own
Her friendship won't survive that test.
I'm so much better as a guest.
Her home I'll treat with reverence
and thoughtfulness and common sense
In every way I'll try to please
– Where did I put her front door keys?

Death wishes

I'd like to die in Bloomingdales,
expire at the Pierre,
Or go in style from the Carlyle
I'd meet my Maker there ...
I could just croak at La Reserve,
collapse at La Coupoule,
or why not go from Deux Magots
with Left Bank in my soul ...
My heart could stop at Skopoulos,
a blue Aegean Isle,
oh perfect Greece, I'd go in peace
to heaven with a smile ...

I've no plans to pass on just yet
in case you're wondering why
it looks as though I wish to go
to find a place to die ...
Well – I was feeling wonderful
I don't think I *looked* ill,
but Lloyds Bank said I could drop dead
and made me make a will ...
That gesture in itself made me
come firmly face to face
with death the act and then the fact
that I should choose the place ...

Death wishes

I mean you're born just *anywhere*,
were you or I consulted?
But I intend to plan my end
and pray God's not insulted ...
I hope he lets me pop off when
I'm suntanned or ecstatic
I couldn't stand to die unplanned
of something undramatic ...
If I expire at the Pierre,
A corpse clutching a menu,
however odd, you'll know that God
agreed the final venue ...

Page Three passions

*P*icture a world where the sex roles were reversed. Try if you can to imagine today's climate in Britain. The instance of appalling rapes and sexual assaults on men would be up by about 30 per cent and 50 per cent in London. Imagine men being left dazed with broken bottles shoved up their rectums, their penises swollen and throbbing with agony after being bitten, crushed or slashed. Can you envisage these men so mentally and physically shattered by the experience that they could not face the thought of sex again? Would they be tremulous, less confident and really fearful about all women, even the gentle ones who cared? No man would ever be able to accept a lift home from a woman because any half-witted fool would be aware that a woman he didn't know well – and come to that even one he did – could be a potential violent attacker who might wield a knife, a gun, or a car jack and threaten to disfigure him for life if he didn't yield to her demands. How would men feel?

Would they start to feel sick about their society and wonder why nothing was being done to protect them, to take their sex seriously, to punish the rapists with sentences that measured up to the horror of their crimes, to give them, the victims, some basic compassion in the court-rooms? Would they be outraged that of the 650 Members of Parliament, 625 of them wore dresses and often high-heeled shoes and sometimes chatted about hair and make-up and bringing up children and there were only 25 men in pin-striped suits? And overwhelmingly it was the women who decided on issues that only affected the men. Would they be horrified if those female MPs laughed and jeered when a man asked for tougher legislation on pictures that offended men? There they'd be, for the most part normal, decent, intelligent, caring, hardworking men –

136

Page Three passions

granted they'd only be earning 73 per cent of what the women earned – and not only would it be difficult to get the women to take them seriously, but the women would laugh good-naturedly if the men insisted they were serious. 'We really like men,' the women would say. 'Of course you're as good as us. Of course we respect you. You've always been equal. Better than us in many cases. You're stronger for one thing.' Into this role-reversed society where men would walk in fear of being viciously attacked by women, sexually assaulted and sometimes left for dead and indeed sometimes murdered – picture male reaction to the Page 3 Boy. Luscious, available, 18- or 19-year-old young men with the most enormous pricks in the world. Page 3 boys wouldn't *do* anything. They'd just stand there and be photographed with their G-strings back to front to show their round appetising balls. And they'd look ripe and ready for sex and half-smile while their enormous cocks stood pert and ready for the stroking.

Page 3 boys would open supermarkets and exhibitions and things, although of course they'd mostly be wearing trousers, but we'd all know what the terrific lumps were nestling under their trousers. Can you imagine female society rewarding to the tune of £100,000 a year a blond guy with an enormous cock – 'He's only just over five feet tall and it must be *11* inches'? Can you see the newspapers doing interviews with the cock-owner? 'I'm not ashamed of my willie,' he'd say. 'I'm from a well-adjusted home and my dad is proud of me.' And the women editors would clamour to talk to Gorgeous George and report to the public that he was, in fact, awfully nice, very bright and he had a good head on his shoulders – if any of you had looked up far enough to notice. There'd be a daily diet of marvellous men with terrifically over-the-top-out-of-proportion pricks. And if any other men had the nerve, the absolute temerity to object, we women would say, 'Oh, come on. You're just jealous just because you haven't got a fabulous pair of balls and a terrific prick.' Could you picture a scene where you would have that sort of conversation with a man? Would men see the Page 3 boys as some sort of attempt to hold them back, keep them in their place? Do you think they might imagine we were being *disrespectful*? In a world where men were being raped, gang-raped and beaten up by people who knew them,

Page Three passions

friends, relatives or just someone on the street who fancied a bit, was
sexually inadequate or didn't have a friendly pair of balls of their own to
fondle, do you think men would unite in their anger that something be
done? Or would there be male columnists saying, 'It's our fault really.
We probably brought it on ourselves. If we'd just been good fathers and
husbands and not insisted on going out to work all this never would have
happened'? Would men mind if amidst the catalogue of rape editorials
they and we were treated to the sight of the passive, available, undressed
Page 3 boys still smiling over their gigantic cocks? 'Have A Real Ding
Dong With Delicious Dave' would invite the *Moon* newspaper. There'd
be a salacious story of two teenage men gang-raped by six violent,
sadistic women a couple of pages later. But men wouldn't connect the
Page 3 boys with the rapes would they? What possible conclusions
could they draw about women not having any respect for men and
wishing to degrade and humiliate them and these cute, smiling boys with
their juicy enormous squeezable pricks? Would men insist that there
was nothing wrong at all in being treated to a daily diet of passive men
with pert erect cocks? The great news for men is that we don't live in a
role-reversed world, the terrific news is that men have deemed it
obscene, pornographic and degrading to publish pictures of the *erect*
penis in *any* periodical or newspaper. They've outlawed publication of
the penis in any newspaper. The great news is that women do not rape
men, generally speaking. Men don't have to hurry home from work
scared that they may be sexually attacked. They are never made to feel
guilty, that in some way it may have been their fault if they are assaulted.
The best news of all is that millions of men who are readers of the *Sun*,
Star and *News of the World* can continue to gaze, for the foreseeable
future, on the topless lovelies, those terrific Page 3 girls. Why should we
women protest? Would men protest if the roles were reversed?

Conclusion

*Y*ou learn to live by living
You learn to give by giving
You learn to fight by fighting
You learn to write by writing
You learn to mate by mating
I am bored to tears with waiting
There's been too much fast living
And I'm sick to death of giving
And I never won at fighting
So I'll persevere with writing.

When a lovely flame dies

I have given up smoking. I don't suppose it interests you very much. It's of little interest to me. Giving up things isn't fascinating. But I have to tell you that, as I stubbed out my last cigarette about six months ago, I told myself it was a sign of the times. I stared at the stub in the brown and white ashtray, the one that has *Buca di Santanonio, Lucca* written on it, and felt nostalgic, wistful, older.

Because I remembered when – and they were different days – cigarettes (dare I say it?) were romantic. They were to do with the mysteries of sex and the fumbling beginnings of sophistication.

My first love affair began on a beach in southern France. I was stretched out in the hazy heat of the Antibes midday sun re-reading *Tender is the Night*. My accessories were a small bikini, blue sunglasses and a packet of Gitanes, lying provocatively half in and half out of my beach bag. There was something urgently attractive and worldly about a person who smoked Gitanes. The rough tobacco was an acquired taste. But then, Gitanes smokers had usually acquired a taste for Sartre and intense conversation. I met 'the man' when I reached for the cigarettes. He appeared to offer me a light. He looked into my eyes and smiled. I inhaled ... and we *knew*.

We dined that evening and the smoke from our cigarettes drifted lazily in the still air of the restaurant garden. A wispy, sensual intermingling. I remember our tanned bodies lying on crumpled sheets with the brilliant blue and white packet of Gitanes next to us. Cigarettes were what you did afterwards. You talked, you stroked, you lingered, you smoked. It's what anyone with even a notion of *savoir faire* did. And it was terrific, I tell you. Simply terrific.

When a lovely flame dies

My first affair stretched over the long French summer and into rusty autumn. Him, me and the Mediterranean-blue and white packet of Gitanes. We did everything together, we discussed practically everything you could think of. Yet the subject of heart disease did not crop up once and in our most intimate moments he never mentioned lung cancer.

Of course I had to change my brand when I came home to England. The Gitanes were too fraught with memories. And, anyway, I needed something warmer-looking to counteract London's leaden skies. Dunhill seemed to suit my mood. The shiny crimson and gold packet. Expensive, traditional, cosseted-looking. I met elegant Dunhill lighters and the men who owned them. Men with Turnbull shirts, dark suits and creative hands.

It was good to sit in Wilton's or the Connaught and gaze first at the menu and then at the packet of Dunhill on the starched tablecloth. Even if you were an absolute gourmet, the crimson and gold packet was a delicious reminder that the best was yet to come. Dunhill men sent flowers, gift-wrapped presents from Bond or Jermyn Street and asked you to marry them. Being English they may not have understood women, but they did appreciate the subtle and wonderful difference between the sexes. These sophisticated smokers did not expect to get a woman on the cheap, either financially or emotionally. The smoking bonded you somehow and they recognised this. It was easy to talk and be romantic while smoke softened the atmosphere. They inhaled and thought what they were going to say, exhaled and said it. Or you did. Dunhills meant dialogue and it was delicious. During the crimson and gold period no one accused anyone of tasting like an ashtray or having hair that reeked of smoke.

Then there were the raunchy, racy Rothmans men. A different breed altogether. Younger, more relaxed, less willing to impress. But very willing to fall in love. They were as sharp and crisp as the navy and white packet. Decisive and enthusiastic. They said, 'Let's.' And you did. You raced to crowded noisy Italian restaurants and to each other's flats and on to planes together – because naturally you had airline tickets to romantic places. And Rothmans were smoked incessantly through all

When a lovely flame dies

the intense interaction. You spent lazy weekends in bed making love, smoking and daring to talk about the rest of your lives. Very sensual and emotional men sometimes blew smoke rings across your body. That was heady stuff. Love, sex, optimism and cigarettes were all mysteriously intertwined.

It was harder to understand people who didn't smoke. They were accepted, of course. We were liberal. But you felt they weren't embracing the good things in life with the same uninhibited fervour as the rest of us. Non-smokers went home a little earlier, drank a lot less and married people who were 'safe'. A non-smoker *never* complained about a smoker. Non-smokers were the very opposite of the macho Marlboro man. He treated his women with a certain rough charm and he was only ever available on his own terms. He handled the sexually aggressive scarlet and white packet with New World nonchalance and he usually used matches. When he wasn't riding cowboy country in Arizona, it was rumoured he was great in bed and amazingly gentle and tender to his Chosen Woman. I never knew one well because I was romantically involved with the Rothmans men. And you get used to a certain brand of man.

Then it happened. The ugly rumours were officially confirmed. Cigarette smoking was Bad for your Health. Overnight it became a dirty, anti-social, lethal habit.

Well, naturally, we all tended to ignore it for a while. Denial is a way of handling grief. Cigarettes *bad* for you? Those pure white, orally gratifying little sticks that were popped into our mouths at every meaningful moment in our lives? Those vital accessories for communication and togetherness? We carried on sucking and blowing and flicking gentle ash and saying it didn't matter. But it did. Next thing you knew was that man after gorgeous man was laying down his cigarettes and saying, 'But not for me.'

Some of the more defiant amongst us persisted for years, but it became an increasingly lonely crusade.

Romantic meals began to die a death. People thought more about their health, their weight, what they were eating and very little about their dining companion. It was hard to get personal over a Perrier and as

When a lovely flame dies

for a cigarette – heaven forbid. Of course you sometimes had the drinks before and during the meal, but the sweet promissory note of a lingering sexual aftermath had vanished. If the topic of sex cropped up and you went home and tried it, there was no sensual chatter afterwards. It seemed that without the curly lazy smoke, the essential *après sex* atmosphere between lovers was not possible. Tender words were left unsaid. Sex, in many cases, became perfunctory.

'What of soul was left, I wonder, when the kissing had to stop?'

Not much, Mr Browning. Not much.

Well, you know the rest. It was only a matter of time before people began to lose interest in sex because sex without romance is depersonalising and depressing. A few people had sex because it was rumoured to be good for you – a form of relaxation and exercise. Heaven help us. Spinach is good for you.

Look, I'm a contemporary, flexible person. My finger, albeit a little wobbly, is on the pulse of modern life. I understand that lung cancer, heart disease and blocked arteries are bad for your health. I read the health columns. It's terrific news that there is a breakthrough for herpes. My spirits soar. It's just that I can't help noticing that sex and cigarettes seemed to go out of fashion at about the same time and I thought I should point out that there seemed to be a very definite connection.

Think what you will, I'm wistful about the bygone era of a drink before and a cigarette after. Those golden days of Rothmans and romance, Gitanes and *je t'aime*. The days when smoke got in your eyes and men lingered over you. That era is finished, gone. Manly men are pumping iron at the local health clubs, getting up early to jog or do press-ups or they're dating other men.

To hell with killer diseases. The fact is I do not want packets of painful nostalgia lying around my flat. I do not want a low tar tug at my memory. Cigarettes remind me of the times that no longer seem to be available to a romantic sensualist.

And I do not wish to be reminded. So I've given up smoking.

Gastronomic tiffs

Sometimes when I get upset
the person in my life gets wet.
Wounding words he's trying to say
are silenced by the Beaujolais.
(Once when it was utter hell
I threw the bloody glass as well.)

Why *do* they say the way they feel
as one's about to start a meal?
All the things he 'won't' and 'can't'
are whispered in the restaurant.
(Others glancing at us two
assume he's saying 'I love you'.)

Years ago a pin-striped chap
got minestrone in his lap
A blond who something ghastly said
received spaghetti on his head.
(It helps to row Italian fashion
Italian waiters do *know* passion.)

In these hard times the vicious quips
are served up with the fish and chips.
But though the words are cruel and odd
I haven't stooped to throwing cod
(I guess my feelings are reserved
for a setting more deserved.)

Gastronomic tiffs

Why is it that the way we live
is founded on the negative?
Any wonder when you *know* things
in frustration that you throw things?
'I can't commit' 'I never plan'
who created Brave New Man?

Funny thing is later on
when rows and years have been and gone
when my love is at an end
and my ex-love is my best friend,
he's *smitten* with the food I hurled
it showed I loved him to the world.

His friends *love* the spaghetti story
bolognese and blood – so gory!
'You *were* adorable and cute –
all that soup down my best suit'.
'Remember when you flung that stew
God, that evening I loved you.'

Forgotten are the private hours
tender moments, pale pink flowers.
All his gentle reminiscings
nought to do with sex and kissing.
So here's the message I'll pass on
food's the recipe for love – THROW ON!

Magic moments

I feel idiotically optimistic. I've just been whirling around the flat and singing along with *Everything's Coming Up Roses*. There are a couple of lines that go, 'Curtain up, light the lights, I've got nothing to hit but the heights' and suddenly I feel like that. No, of course the feeling won't last. I'm a mild manic depressive. But the ups are wonderful.

Nothing in life has changed. Except the sofas are covered and I bought a dishwasher on interest-free credit. Well, there are a couple of men in the pipeline with semi-possibilities and I'm starting to flirt again. Look, I don't know what the possibilities are. It's not exactly the time in social and viral history to rush headlong into an affair. And I never was big on headlong. I'll say this for AIDS, it's a great equaliser. For once the men I meet are as wary as me. But sex is in the air, probably the best place for it, and I'm doing just fine over lunches, funny dinners, late night conversations and quirky phone calls.

No, it's not dull, it's rather romantic in a 1987 sort of way. Yes I do admit that sex with someone I loved was my favourite way to spend time. Of *course* I can remember spending weekends in bed with my lover and maybe just getting up in time to make it to Europa Foods before it closed on Saturday evening. I loved all that. But to be honest, when I think of the magic moments, if you'll excuse the corny expression, they're more to do with revelation or the sweet realisation that life can be wonderful sometimes. They're rarely about great sex. I honestly can't recall the details of great sex any more than I can remember exactly how great pain felt. I just know I've had my share of both and they were frequently connected.

Yet I remember with absolute clarity the first time I saw the sunrise at

Magic moments

Villefranche. I was in a small boat and I'd sailed around from Nice at about four o'clock one May morning with the man who was to become my first lover. I remember that first sight of the sun creeping over the horizon and filling the Mediterranean sky with a blaze of morning glory. Robert, my Frenchman, stood with his arm around my shoulder. The waves gently lapped the little boat and across the water I could see the fishermen at the harbour café, their nets draped along the shore. I loved France with a passion then, and I couldn't believe I was free to see the triumphant dawning of such a day with such a man. It seemed a private memory to treasure, a personal best. But years later I came across a passage in a book by Evelyn Waugh. He'd written that every time he was tempted to use the word 'beautiful' he'd compare what he was about to describe with the sunrise at Villefranche. And if it didn't match up he didn't use it. Maybe that moment was so good because that's when I suspected I was going to fall in love. The time just before you sense you're going to abandon yourself to another human being is very pleasurable.

I remember being with a man I adored on a small beach in Crete one late September. We were lazy, tanned and sitting on a small wooden jetty with our feet in the clear water. He stared down at our wriggling toes and said, 'Only another 48 hours to go.' And we both smiled and winced at being torn away at this time out of time to return home to London. But there was that day back home when we agreed we had to meet for lunch even though we could only spare one brief hour. He dashed off to one pub and I rushed off to another because lovers don't always listen to directions. Ah, but we had a moment, literally, when we finally met up in the Windsor Castle in Campden Hill, gazed at each other and said in agonising unison, 'I have to go now.'

I remember sitting on the top deck of a languid ferry as it steamed out of a Yugoslav port on its way to Zagreb. Gosh, I'd fallen in love again. But this time, for the first time ever, I thought I'd like to marry the man. He proposed. I mean I thought he did. Turning towards me he said 'And how would you like to be the third Mrs. H?' Well, no, it didn't quite have the ring of fresh young love I'd always promised myself and I did *say* that it made me feel like Second-hand Rose. I don't know what was

Magic moments

wrong with 'Will you marry me?' But H always did things his own special way. Still, I did feel a smile seeping through my body and I was intensely happy. Some time later when I thought I'd accept the proposal and you know, just mention it again, H said absent-mindedly, 'Oh no. I said "*would* you", not *will* you. I just wanted to know how you felt and if you would marry me if it came to the crunch.' H and I had language difficulties for years.

I did love our moments in cheap caffs where they do the best egg, bacon and chips in the world. Once we met at midday in Piccadilly with him looking grey flannel elegant and me looking breathtakingly ordinary. He watched me struggling with the tomato ketchup and said it was odd that I couldn't manage the simple things in life. He took the bottle from me and opened it with one swift turn of the bottle top. A jet of tomato ketchup hit the wall and flew off down the side of his face and all the way down the front of his impeccable suit. I didn't mean to laugh. It's just that he had been looking so manful and sophisticated and ketchup can really cut a man down to size. He said he didn't know why we kept coming to such dreadful places. But when the waitress had sponged his suit and he'd eaten his meal he said it was, after all, lovely to see me and yes, he did love cheap caffs provided you were wearing the right clothes. As we left he hugged me in the street and said, 'You know, that was a marvellous lunch.'

Once I was working in Italy and they had a national rail strike on the day I was due to travel from Milan to Florence. There was pandemonium at the central station where dozens of coaches had been laid on to replace the trains. My suitcase was heavy, I couldn't see a single coach whose destination was Firenze and grown men and little old ladies were acting with undue violence around me. I tell you I despaired in the early morning heat as I *had* to be in Florence for an afternoon appointment. A tall man with an attractive, reassuring face spoke to me in French. He, too, had to get to Florence. 'You guard the cases and I'll find a coach and we'll fight our way through the crowds together,' he said. Within half an hour we were on our way and as the coach sped through the Italian countryside I had one of the nicest most intimate conversations I've ever had with a total stranger. He said it was funny about

Magic moments

travelling alone because you never were alone unless you wanted to be. Here's you and I locked in conversation, he said, and there's nowhere else I'd rather be.

I was alone when I crossed the Columbia campus for the first time one freezing January day in New York. Hundreds of students who seemed to know where they were going yelled at each other and clustered in groups that first day of term. I remember pulling my coat around me tightly and thinking I don't care if no-one talks to me just so long as I can be here. It was the University I hadn't had at eighteen and I was so *thrilled* as I made my way across the icy paths to enrol. In May of that year I was sprawled on the campus grass waiting for Erich and other friends to arrive. The air was warm and I remember gazing at the magnolia tree that grew near Ferris Booth Hall where we all met for lunches. The tree had straggled through winter to blossoming pink beauty. Next time you bloom, I thought, I won't be in New York to see you. There was the night Erich dyed his blond hair black just to prove to me that blonds didn't have more fun and he was seriously attractive *whatever* his hair colour. I don't know why it was such a great evening. Maybe it was the absurdity of it all. There was Erich doing his usual leap over the subway turnstile and flirting wildly with whoever he landed nearest. But this Saturday evening no one responded. His reception at our favourite bars and hangouts in Greenwich Village was unmemorable. His cute conversation went unheeded, his winks and grins were ignored. But Erich-like he did have the grace to laugh. 'I can't believe this Marce,' he said, 'You'd think blond was all I'd *got*. I'm gonna remember this.' And as we sat close and giggling in the crowded bar and a bunch of young, out-of-work Broadway actors burst into song, I thought that I'd probably remember the evening too. The hair dye took weeks to come out. Erich is coming to stay with me this month.

Although I've spent years confusing love and friendship with men – who the hell knew what they were offering? – sometimes I hit lucky. I had a moment when David hugged me briefly and said tenderly for an Australian that it was possible to have an affair with someone without having an affair. Crocodile Dundee made me very sentimental I can tell you.

Magic moments

I suppose you 'fall in love' with women in a way, although it doesn't feel quite the same. You do have moments with them that are very precious. I don't collect photos but I have all kinds of memory pictures of them that are wonderful. Jackie, beautiful and precocious, giggling at a Charity Ball at the Dorchester when we met in our teens; Bonnie, curled up in front of the fire at the farmhouse in New Jersey; Francoise leaping to catch a beach ball, dark tan and strong limbed and wearing a white bikini; Jeanne giving us all Easter baskets tied with ribbon and filled with presents; Rebecca planting the heather on my terrace so I'd remember her when she was gone; Joan beaming in hospital the day after Katharine was born; Jo, striding across the heath one shiny autumn day, saying we were mad not to do this more often; Elaine, adorable and curvy, cleaning the kitchen floor in her skimpy underwear when we shared a flat and my date saying, 'Now who's that?'; Pattie being late for work so she could give me breakfast and sympathy while I sobbed and her saying some men weren't worth it and me feeling suddenly better.

Gosh, I know I'm being sentimental and this is sounding rather late-night mellow and over-the-top, but this is an article about the sweet bits of life. Any fool can dwell on the rest. Ndojmg bkdiling kne. XXXX? ILBODC!!! Blast. Damn. Hell. I don't *believe* this. The Electricity board really know how to kill a mood. There's just been a power failure and it's about one in the morning and I'm furious. Well, I mean I'm put out. *You* try typing by candlelight. It's hard to hold an optimistic, sentimental mood when you can't find a box of matches. Two neighbours have just knocked on the door and said what was I doing about it – I mean, what are they doing up at this hour? And Georgina just rang and said she *knew* I wouldn't be asleep and she'd been to a party and two men said they were wearing wellies these days which in case I didn't know meant condoms. She'd asked another man if he wore wellies and he said wellies you must be joking, I'm wearing waders. Oh God, what's the world coming to? Where's the lousy Tipp-Ex? My train of thought has crashed. I'm going to bed. Sod magic moments.

Except I just remembered that last time there was a power failure I was with someone at his Battersea flat and he was playing a guitar softly and candlelight seemed more than adequate...

Ark-ache

To Noah it probably was a lark
inviting couples on his ark,
but every hearty hostess since
has followed Noah's duo hints.

'Do come on Thursday if you can
I seem to have an extra man ...'
She usually neglects to say
the extra man is deeply gay.

This crazy 'two-by-two' obsession
causes in us great depression.
Half the time we're only eating
'cos we even up the seating.

It seems that 7, 5 or 9
could ruin food and vintage wine.
A hostess in an evening whirl
won't contemplate a 'single' girl.

An extra man's potential fun
an extra female isn't 'done'.
Is she boring or a threat
no one has discovered, yet.

I'm sure that when we're very old
and all attraction has gone cold
parties will be given for us
and everyone will quite adore us.

Ark-ache

'You *must* meet her she's wise and witty
at eighty-five she's still quite pretty.'
We'll stagger in if we're still able
and be the *seventh* at the table.

Dear odd number, triumph sweet
a single lady asked to eat ...
So bite your lip and no more tears
you'll be a wow in sixty years.

Will Gym fix-it?

*W*hat am I doing here? Why did I come? Why are there forty of us? What made me imagine this would be a small select group? Why was I too mean to buy new gym shoes? Why does that black girl next to me look so terrific in her satin shorts? Why are my toes so far away? What does the Eva Braun instructress mean 'do that thirty times'? Why do I have a shooting pain in my left thigh? Who said twenty-four sit-ups were easy? Why can't I breathe properly? Why do we have to push our bodies just that little bit further? Why are we running round this floor? Does she know I never breathe through my nose? Why are other people overtaking me? Is that my heart attacking me? Is there a doctor in the house? What good can this possibly be doing me? Why is she so relentless? Why do I feel I have gatecrashed the training programme for the Olympics? Can we stop this lunacy? Why is my leg supposed to bend effortlessly behind me? How do I overcome sharp cramp? Can I get out of this position? What if I have to stay here for hours? What was that awful crack? Doesn't it feel g-o-o-d to have the use of my left leg again? Since when have press-ups been OK for women? Is she kidding, 'do forty of them'? Why can't I do *one*? Oh God, what are they doing now? Why is everyone facing the other way? Why are we doing more sit-ups? What is happening to the lower part of my abdomen? Will this ruin my child-bearing chances? Could my uterus drop out? Could I drop out? Would she notice? Has that person fainted? Why isn't she allowed water? Why aren't I allowed water? Do I really want a new body? What is wrong with the one I have? Have I been inundated with personal complaints? Why am I so seduced by the words 'physical fitness'? Why did I pay good money to come here and be tortured? Why are we pounding round the room the other way? Am I

Will Gym fix-it?

supposed to see things differently? Will this improve my sex-life? Does having a flat stomach and slender thighs mean desirable men will leap out of taxis and jump on me? Does Eva Braun get jumped on? Doesn't she know I'll be rigid as a board for days? What happens if I have a hot date tomorrow? Will he understand that I won't be able to move a muscle? Why is everyone so obsessed with exercise classes? Does Jane Fonda really do this every day? How come that black girl can do everything? What is slipping? Is that a disc or my pants? How is it I didn't know I had so many muscles lying dormant? Shouldn't I leave them lying dormant? Why can't we rest for one lousy moment? What are my chances of a refund on this course? Will my medical insurance cover the damage I've done? Why don't I take a course on flower arranging?

On loving and loathing clothing

*W*hy are clothes so *important*? I mean apart from the fact that they keep you warm and cover up bits of you that have to be covered otherwise you'd be arrested. Why, when I consider myself to be a reasonably intelligent, secure person (listen, you didn't know me *before*), do I spend so much time agonising over what to wear? It was so much easier when I was broke and in my first job. I only had a couple of dresses, two pairs of trousers, a navy sweater and a pair of shoes that went with absolutely everything. Who am I kidding? It was always hell. I never knew what to buy and I never knew what to wear. The problem is you know, you just damn well *know*, that the world is nicer to you when you're well dressed. It's no good asking *me* what the right clothes are. It's not that I don't accidentally *buy* them sometimes. But I'm never sure when it is right to *wear* them. Look, things aren't so bad that I can't go out. I get to work and stuff like that and only last week I met a man I know near the tomatoes in Marks and Spencer. He took one look at my jacket and my pale blue thick cotton shirt and my superbly shrunk jeans and my brown shoes. Oh, and the Zandra Rhodes socks I won in the office raffle. They're sort of mauve and white and stripy. A fiendishly subtle combination I always feel. And this attractive man said, 'Well. *Hello*. Where are you *going*?' This is always a clue to the fact that you don't look ordinary. I am relating this incident to convey to you that I am the kind of person who can, should the situation arise, look stunning near a vegetable counter. It was one of those rare moments when my outfit and I happened to gell. But could I

On loving and loathing clothing

look *intentionally* well dressed? Er. No. The trouble is, well, one of the troubles is that, everyone knows clothes give away all sorts of clues as to who you are and what you do and even what you are thinking. Life is easy, clotheswise, when you're not doing anything or thinking about very much. Most of the time I don't want my clothes to *say* anything. Being comfortable, anonymous and getting my hair to do *something* other than cling to my head in fine desperation is about the height of my ambition on an average day. It's not the kind of look calculated to startle the neighbours or my workmates. Men don't leap out of taxis or bound across crowded rooms saying 'I just had to meet you.' My general appearance signals very clearly 'Leave me alone.'

This may not seem much to you but it's taken me years to perfect this technique. Blending in does not happen overnight. When you've straggled up from Leigh-on-Sea without a sartorial *clue*, blending in is a personal triumph. I've collected quite a few suits over the past few years and if push came to shove I could go out for a drink after work, although dinner might be expecting too much. Particularly if the man was. I've never located those clothes you read about that are meant to fly you confidently through a working day and then, at least according to all those magazine photographs, you take off a simple black jacket to reveal an urgent strappy number in pale cream that makes him sigh. Real people don't do that. If I have a hot date, well, say a warm dinner with someone interesting, I have to rush home from work and soak in the bath and really *think* what I want my clothes to say.

It's quite hard to strike the right combination of socio-economic acceptability, international chic, mysterious sex-appeal and just a dash of wit. My crinkly gold strapless dress just passes muster provided I add a Calvin Klein belt and a paper hat. It may seem odd to you, but three New Year's Eves ago that outfit seemed to work. No, of course I haven't worn it again. I bought it because it was in a sale and I was going through a phase of knowing what I wanted to say and having the courage to say it. There was a sensual, humorous message I wanted to get across. Was I desperate or in love? I was both. You think a person in a normal frame of mind buys a dress like that?

But if people are reading things into my clothes I have to be careful

On loving and loathing clothing

what I am saying. What *do* you wear to convey intelligent, likes to be well treated, adores work but realises there is more to life, likes men but doesn't want to spend every waking moment trying to please them, likes women and never wants to alienate them, will happily eat in the Ritz Grill and any good transport caff, likes sex but not necessarily at this very minute, likes clothes but doesn't think they matter, except when they do?

I used to buy clothes for a social life and smuggle a few of the more toned-down numbers into my work life. Now I buy clothes for work and hope to hell that no one suddenly asks me to a wedding, a party, a dinner, or a cocktail party in SW1 – although I could manage Hampstead. A feeling of controlled panic runs through me when I'm asked anywhere special. It's so wonderful to be *invited*, but I can't face looking in the wardrobe. It holds the darkest secrets of my soul, some aching memories, 28 pairs of shoes, six grey sweaters and not a single decent black belt. I've never been able to throw away people, books or clothes. Well, this year I have made a bit of an effort and said goodbye to three men but it doesn't solve the wardrobe problem. Yes of *course* I'm getting asked out less and you could say that that was a help. But you couldn't call it positive fashion action, could you?

I do try to adopt the positive shopping approach, but I really don't believe that maxim about trying on clothes when you're looking and feeling good. I have skipped down Bond Street in a suntanned, slender zip of a mood and tried on stuff I thought I could never wear and looked wonderful – in the shop. My scarlet jacket with the padded shoulders, the Italian cotton suit that the assistant said looked important. Maybe next time I come back from Skiathos and I've fallen in love and I'm a size 8 I'll be able to wear them ... until then they're on permanent loan to skinny friends and well-wishers. Conversely, I was in a state of terminal *depression* when I bought my outsize navy blue wool and cashmere coat – but I wore it pratically every day from February to June and it looks good and covers all the confusion underneath. But I do run into serious trouble when I'm trying on clothes and I think now what does this *go* with. What my grey sweaters mostly match is the other grey sweaters.

It mystifies me that friends can *plan* what to wear on a special day

On loving and loathing clothing

because even *supposing* they've got the right clothes, how on earth do they know what *they* are going to be looking like, feeling like on the day. I have about as much control over the shape of my face, the state of my skin, the fullness of my hair, the roundness of my stomach and the cheerfulness of my mood as I have over the weather. Also, how do you look well dressed and relaxed without it appearing that you've gone to a whole lot of effort? it would be awful if people thought you'd actually *worried* about your clothes.

Now you may think I'm confused about my clothes, but where I'm *brilliant* is in my choice of women friends. Take Jackie. She's not only warm and funny but she's the same size as me and *her* clothes make me look and feel sensational. And I'm not such a complete idiot when it comes to fashion. It encourages me enormously that both Amanda and Cindy borrow *my* clothes and they look terrific in them. Oh, I suppose things might improve as I get to be an old lady. I'll probably be *soignée* as hell in my seventies. Death worries me though. As Woody Allen said, 'Eternal nothingness is OK if you're dressed for it.'

Long-distance lament

*W*ell, Paul is moving house this week
Jo's staying with her mother
Annette barely has time to speak
Since she's met A N Other

Selwyn's feeling rough again
He said Love is a menace
Joan is catching some smart train
that goes Express to Venice

Peter has a baby girl
Says fatherhood is dizzy
Viv is in a wedding whirl
And very very busy

I could ask Ann & John I s'pose
Of course there's always Leni
But how she'd find the time God knows
I can't get through to Jennie

My former lover says he can't
His life is far to frantic
He's opened a new restaurant
And hates calls trans-Atlantic

I've such good friends – yet I must say
that confidence can waver
If you're three thousand miles away
and phone to ask a favour

Long-distance lament

'Friends are sacred,' Elaine cried
'So guard 'em, keep 'em, feed 'em
I did. How come they're occupied
the one damn time I need 'em?

Those good, crazy people, my married friends

*W*e've come to an understanding, my married friends and I. Nobody gets it right. At least not all of the time. We don't quite understand how we have come to be living the way we are. In some ways our lives are far better than we'd hoped. In other ways worse. And all of us get wistful sometimes. But we more or less lead the lives that suit us even if at times we live in a dreadfully unsuitable fashion. We have different highs and lows but I've noticed that they seem to eat regularly whatever's happening.

I like the idea of falling in love and they like the idea of staying married. All our chances seem slim sometimes, 'You're so brave,' they say to me. 'Fancy doing all that alone.' 'You're so stoic,' I say to them. 'Imagine going through all that with someone.' But being close to them has broken down many of my prejudices about marriage. I confess I never had any illusions. The possibilities of being happy seem to be the same whether you're married or single. 'You just pick your own disabilities,' said my married friend John.

They treat me as part of the family. 'Of *course* you'll be coming down over Easter.' I'm the errant child, 'Now sit down and eat all your food', the teenager, 'Is *that* what people are wearing?'; the therapist, 'I've simply got to talk to you about Bonnie'; the sexual libertine, 'You can sleep with a different man every night'; the speaker of wisdom and truth, 'You do see things so clearly'; the nun 'How come you don't mind not having sex?'; the fool, 'You're mad to live like that'; the threat, 'It's obvious Amanda will get ideas spending time with you'; the benign aunt, 'The kids would adore to spend a week with you'; the Samaritan, 'Can you come over? I'm desperate' and even an intimate date, 'Isn't it *marvellous* just the three of us?'

On my side I have to say I do love them very much. It's perfectly

Those good, crazy people, my married friends

obvious that their married lives would survive without me, but I do wonder what my single life would have been like without them. I remain fascinated by their togetherness and their strange separateness and by the endless knocks their marriages can survive.

Once or twice the insights into their lives have been so grim that I've fled home, flopped on the sofa, called a single friend and said 'Don't do it. Don't ever do it. It's hell I tell you. Sheer hell.' Once I stayed with two of them who were going through what she called 'a difficult patch'. One balmy June evening I was on my way out for dinner when I heard their raised voices coming from the bedroom. I hesitated at the front door of the flat. 'And I'd like to stick a knife into you very slowly and watch the blood ooze into the carpet,' she was saying. I raced down the corridor and into their room. 'Er . . . you don't think that one of you would like to come and have dinner with me?' I said. And she did. 'Stay single,' she muttered over the watercress soup.

But there was that Thanksgiving Day in New York when I arrived to find two of my favourite married friends snugly wrapped in their white towelling dressing gowns. The children aged four and two were being held up to the windows to watch the great Macy's parade as it wended its noisy colourful way along Central Park West. Maybe it was the American sentimentality of it, maybe it was the smells of the turkey Thanksgiving lunch coming from the kitchen, maybe it was the way everyone hugged each other and shrieked and yelled as Mickey Mouse and Pluto ballooned past, maybe it was the way four-year-old Katharine kissed me and put her small hand in mine. I'll never know. All I know is that in the crowded family warmth of their living-room I suddenly felt solitary and single and I knew I'd got it terribly wrong. I wiped a couple of hot tears from my eyes and said, 'It's funny how I always cry at parades.'

Both the married women friends and the married men friends communicate brilliantly with me but they frequently have terrible problems communicating with each other. It's not always easy being an interpreter but I keep thinking that it's good practice. 'Will you for God's sake explain to her that I don't want more children?'; 'He listens to you. Tell him his manic tidiness and food fixations are driving me mad'; 'Tell her if

Those good, crazy people, my married friends

she doesn't lose some weight I'm leaving'; 'Go on. Tell him he's boring and possessive'; 'Will you kindly explain to my wife about money'; '*You* tell him about his friends'; 'Could you sort of tell her that I'm very sorry and I didn't mean it'; 'Please explain intimacy to him'; Such statements are invariably made in the presence of the partner and they both then glare at me while I stutter out my hopefully more acceptable version.

It's obvious that sometimes three's company and two's a crowd but I do have to cover some dangerous conversational ground. And then I'm the audience that gives someone courage to speak the unspeakable. 'What would you do,' said one of my friends as he, his wife and I were cosily sipping our hot chocolate in front of the fire on a crackly autumn weekend, 'if you knew your wife was sleeping with another man?' I've tried muttering that in my case such an event would be extremely unlikely and God knows if I could find a wife I'd put up with practically anything. But I always add a range of practical options so whoever asks the question knows that I'm taking things seriously. 'I'd beat her up, or beat the lover up, or have an affair myself, or emigrate, or try a new after-shave, or maybe I'd talk about it every single meal time and bedtime for the next six months or threaten suicide or take up pot-holing.'

To be honest it isn't altogether unknown for my married friends to have er ... dalliances outside their marriages. Normally after, say, five years together, someone is up to something. But not in every case. Yet in some curious way the flirtations, because they are rarely serious, seem to strengthen their marriages. There are showdowns and sudden midweek lunches, tears and intense conversations and I'm summoned to explain to him/her how much she/he really loves the other one. The tension means a frantic renewal of their sex lives and then life settles down as before, give or take a few bits of smashed household equipment. And in one case a new baby. It's wonderful stuff. I marvel at it constantly. The married men friends are very touching at such threatening moments. They not only beg for advice but treat me as if I'm sterling marriage material and quite forget they ever criticised me. 'You wouldn't behave like that,' they say mournfully.

Married women friends have been known to flee to my flat for what

Those good, crazy people, my married friends

they call peace and quiet. We play the stereo loudly, the phone rings constantly and other people have been known to drop by. 'I could live like this,' they say. 'It's great to be *alone* isn't it?'

I find that my married friends have enormous difficulty in grasping the concept of alone. By their definition, anyone who isn't married is alone.

Their statements on their lives are particularly helpful when it comes to my sorting out any confusion in my mind about getting married and having children. 'I never thought I'd be this secure and happy and having a child is the best thing I ever did.' 'You have to be married in order to realise it isn't necessary and you have to have children in order to realise that you don't need them.' I'm glad I asked. When their marriages are going through periods of calm and sweet contentment, they try to fix me up. 'You ought to try getting married Marce,' they say as though marriage were this season's dress I might slip on for size and fit. Amanda thinks I need a nice steady Norfolk farmer. Philip, who's divinely non-critical and very optimistic about *his* sex and also very selective about mine, has introduced me to some marvellous interesting men. There was the alcoholic surgeon – 'He never drinks before he operates'; the gay writer – 'You could probably talk him out of it'; the Danish industrialist – 'He and his wife haven't got on for years' and the TV reporter who was wildly in love with someone else – 'But you're much more his type'. Ann and John keep praising the virtues of my friend Selwyn. Barbara and David keep saying I really ought to marry a nice Australian. And Joan gets positively irate that H and I don't settle down together. 'I know he's bloody impossible,' she rants down the phone, 'but let's face it, you're perfect for each other.'

When my single life takes off into unexpected orbit their attitudes towards me and their own lives tend to change. 'I'd give anything in the world to be in love again'; 'Are you *really* flying to meet him in Sri Lanka?'; 'You do have the most amazing life'; 'No wonder my wife thinks I'm dull'; 'You'll never get married if you keep living like this'; 'Why can't you live a normal life like the rest of us?'

'Give me a break,' I say, as I gaze happily at their homes, their kids, their familiar married clutter that is so dear to me.

Those good, crazy people, my married friends

'All right then,' say the women in particular, 'but we want to hear all about it. Every *detail*.'

They're unfailingly hospitable to any man I bring along to meet them, but I can't imagine why I thought it was easier to introduce a man in your life to your married friends than to your family.

'I liked him Marce,' said Philip through gritted teeth one Sunday evening in Sussex when the man had departed. 'Just because he broke my wine glass, blocked the lavatory and beat me at tennis, I don't want you to think that I didn't like him.'

'He hated him,' said Joan warmly as we settled down in the garden chairs for our usual inquest on a summer weekend, 'But I thought he was gorgeous.'

Blissfully and happily, my married friends forget my gender. 'What would you like for a present if you were a woman?' Anthony asked me a week before Jackie's birthday. 'You'll never guess what,' said Joan. 'Mrs. Hughes down the road thought Philip had a *woman* in the house when I was away one weekend'. So I said, 'Don't be silly, it was you.' And Barbara said 'It's daft David going off to the Greek Islands with all those unattached women lying around. Don't you think it would be a good idea if he went with you instead?'

Three years ago when I was rather ill in hospital, the married friends and the single friends rallied around magnificently. The single ones squeezed my hand, whispered in my ear, 'Of course you're going to be OK,' and empathised like single survivors. The married ones carried on as alarmingly as fraught parents, each couple insisting that I stayed with them because they could offer the best post-operative facilities. 'It's quieter at our place'; 'We've got a lift in our block'; 'There's that perfect little bedroom waiting for you'; 'We've got staff and you'll be waited on hand and foot', 'It will be a *privilege* to have you'. I tell you, I loved it. I lay back in my narrow bed watching them squabbling over me and I felt wonderful. My mother was out of the country on holiday, my difficult lover was forgotten. I was surrounded by those good crazy people my married friends. They insisted on telling me it was awful that I should find myself *alone* at a time like this. What did I expect? They never did understand the meaning of the word.

Note to the Editor

*B*revity is the soul of wit
and I am most aware of it
but Editors are quite absurd
they pay you by the bloody word.

Though with brief humour
I am smitten, succinct
swift quips do not get
written as impecunious I
am I ramble on ad nauseam

So *au revoir petits bon mots*,
A girl must think of her cash flow.
I'll have a literary success
when Eds pay more if I write less.

Ugh, awful, who wants sex with a man?

*H*ere it is at last. The book you've all been waiting for. A wonderful addition to the a-little-of-what-you-fancy-will-probably-kill-you trend that is so much a part of life in the 'Eighties. The book is called *Sex Is Not Compulsory* by Liz Hodgkinson. Sex, by the way, obviously *is* compulsory if you want to sell books, otherwise this book might be called *Celibacy – The Only Way To Live*. But then few people would be interested and no one would buy it.

Liz Hodgkinson is a happily married woman in her forties and has a reputation as an intelligent writer on health-related topics. But you know how it is. Liz realised after years of marriage that sex was not so sexy any more. And she thought about it and discussed it with her husband. They realised that although they liked each other there was no longer a sexual attraction. And so by mutual consent they decided not to have sex. Gosh. What a complete *surprise*. Could there be another couple in the whole of *Britain* who don't have sex after 20 years of marriage? 'Sex,' she says, 'apart from its essential purpose of reproduction is ultimately an unproductive and time-wasting activity.' Strike me, I never thought of it like that. You know I thought I was *enjoying* myself. But there was I rolling around with a man wasting time dammit. Also, according to Liz, 'Most women prefer to talk and exchange ideas rather than groping around in messy body contact.' Ugh, awful, disgusting, take it away, who'd want sex with a man? How could a decent, intelligent woman like me have stooped to anything so shudderingly *tacky*? Liz tackles the question that has been worrying the hell out of

Ugh, awful, who wants sex with a man?

lovers down the centuries. 'Does sexual desire really exist?' She's *convinced* that if certain well-known creative people can live without being sexually aroused, then so can you. You see, if you've got an active fulfilled life you can have 'long-term contentment' – provided, of course, you *don't* have sex. She cites as celibate role models Andy Warhol, Jesus Christ, Cliff Richard and Virginia Woolf. It's obviously very easy for you to identify with a partying painter, the Son of God, an ageing pop star and the genius from the Bloomsbury set. Still it's comforting to think Virginia, on account of never having sex with Leonard, did at least enjoy 'long-term contentment' before she committed suicide.

OK. You're not convinced that giving up sex is a good idea? You still want to do it? You know *men* who want to do it? Do they not *know*, pleads Liz, that frequent sex may cause them to become deficient in zinc, now recognised as one of *the* essential trace minerals? Not enough zinc can cause illness, depressive conditions and infertility. And no, you *can't* do it yourself. Masturbation, which also depletes zinc levels, can cause – you guessed it – failing eyesight. Gosh, Liz will stop at nothing to put us off sex and I'm hoping the office won't read too much into my wearing glasses. In the chapter on *Celibacy and Health* Liz writes feelingly on the diseases we're all going to get if we have messy body contact with a man. Gonorrhoea, syphilis, genital herpes, cystitis, hepatitis B plus the stern warning that AIDS will eventually kill off two-thirds of humanity. And, by the way, if you *think* or indeed have ever *thought* that you were in love, boy did you get *that* wrong. Liz assures us, 'People always and only fall in love when they are impatient with their present way of life and want to establish something dramatically different.' Women who have sex with men, she says, are being 'exploited'. Was it really like that for Andrew and Fergie? Is he exploiting her? Will his eyesight fail? Will Liz be writing to the Palace to implore them to *stop* before they both fall very ill? And how about *you*? Did you ever melt into a man's arms feeling positively wonderful? Liz can't think why. 'For a woman, however one likes to look at it, sexual intercourse constitutes a form of attack.' I may be a bit slow in some respects but I think I could spot the difference between a welcome lover and rapist. Liz observes that women

Ugh, awful, who wants sex with a man?

do not want to be raped (score 10 out of 10 for real perception there Liz) but they *do* want to attract men. It's obvious to her that 'a woman's right to sexual fulfilment and the rising rape figures go hand in hand.' She knows how *difficult* it is for rapists. 'A confused man cannot be expected to know the difference between a woman who wants it and one who does not. By insisting that we are sexual creatures we have, in some way, invited ourselves to be raped.' Well said. Liz has the makings of some of our High Court Judges, doesn't she?

So what are you going to do, you sexual females out there, if you do not want to be raped, catch deadly diseases or spread them. Well you could enter a nunnery. 'Monks and nuns in religious communities are mostly very happy and *they live longer* than their peers in the outside world.' This has nothing to do with the fact that their lives are ordered and peaceful. Gosh no. Surely you didn't think *that*. And nuns don't get cervical cancer. 'Sexually promiscuous women and prostitutes' (Liz lumps them together in one sentence, is she trying to tell you something?) 'are greatly at risk.' No, Liz, in fairness, makes it clear that you don't *have* to become a nun but she'd like you to live like one.

Liz Hodgkinson's book will probably sell. I must say it would make a marvellous present to *all* married women who might like to pass it on to their husbands when they've run out of excuses not to have sex. Anyone permanently impotent will probably appreciate it and so will all women disillusioned with men and life. Such people will be able to clutch this little volume to them secure in the knowledge that falling in love is a waste of time, and sex, whatever the circumstances, is irrelevant and dangerous. God knows, you may agree with her.

Sexclusive interview

COSMO Good to meet you Sex. It's so nice of you to agree to be interviewed.

SEX Listen, I'm so thrilled that someone decent is still talking to me. You're not worried about me being seen in your office are you?

COSMO Goodness no. Lots of people seem to assume you run the place. Your influence is on every page they tell us.

SEX Is that so?

COSMO No, it isn't so. But that's what they tell us. Let's say we've given you some very enthusiastic write-ups in the past.

SEX Those were the days. People still like to read about me? I mean, are they still interested?

COSMO Well people are always very curious about you even if they claim not to be. But we sense a change of attitudes. Do you detect this?

SEX Are you crazy? That would be like being in Parliament Square and not detecting Big Ben. I may be paranoid but I think that lots of people are monumentally opposed to me these days.

COSMO How do you feel about that?

SEX How do I feel? Terrible is how I feel. I'm soldiering on but it's not easy. I've lost weight, I take tranquillizers and I'm seeing a psychiatrist three times a week. She says I've lost my self-esteem. Listen, I know I'm terribly important. But I do crave social approval and I'm simply not getting it any more.

COSMO Tell us why you're important.

SEX Are you kidding? I mean, I only keep the human race going. If I quit that's the end of life on this planet isn't it? And apart from that, what about the *pleasure* I give people? Doesn't anybody remember anything when they're bad-mouthing me? Lots of people have had lots of won-

Sexclusive interview

derful moments because of me. Don't any of your readers like me? Don't tell me no, I may have a cardiac arrest.

COSMO You can relax. It seems that the overwhelming majority think that at best you're terrific. But they are concerned about Love. Ideally they would like both of you.

SEX *They're* concerned about Love? Me too. You think I'm insensitive? I'm crazy about Love. We're the best double act in town. I mean sheer magic. Sensational. You're talking top of the bill for millions of years there.

COSMO Then tell us why you make so many solo appearances. You still do a lot of one night stands, don't you?

SEX Sure. I'm a professional. I have to keep going. My brief is the show must go on with or without Love. You think it's sad people want me without Love? Sometimes I think it's tragic. What do you want me to do? Hibernate? I've got a job to do.

COSMO What do you think of the publicity you've been getting recently? Does bad press still affect you? Or have you grown used to criticism over the years?

SEX Affect me? You bet your *Cosmo* world it affects me. That's what's getting to everyone isn't it? They're trying to kill me out there. Who knows what's going on? One moment I'm a hit, I'm wonderful. They bring out books like *The Joy of Sex* – they were good times. Now my name's dirt. All I do, if you read the papers, is transmit disease, get teenagers pregnant, cause marriages to break up. I tell the psychiatrist I'm trash suddenly.

COSMO Do you think that maybe you went slightly over the top in recent years? You were strutting your stuff. Perhaps it was a case of over-exposure?

SEX Is that my fault? People wanted me. I'm not a complicated person. Listen, I take some understanding. I can be a bit racy I admit. I have to be controlled. When I'm having fun and people are enjoying me and saying I'm terrific and my name is in lights well – maybe it's true I took advantage. Maybe you caught my act? If I say so myself I was a sensation.

COSMO We caught your act. You *were* wonderful. You know some-

Sexclusive interview

times we get so wistful just thinking about how good you were. By the way did you wink just then?

SEX Well you're kind of glossy and good looking. You seem interested in me. You know for a brief moment I was starting to feel good again.

COSMO Oh we know the feeling. It is nice to have someone wink at you. At least you still have the sense of humour to flirt. You do know how much we need you, don't you?

SEX Need, schmeed. Damn sure the world needs me. I want to be *liked*. I want a few rave reviews again. It's been hell. Nobody knows the troubles I've seen. My press cuttings stink. Even you, *Cosmo*. I've noticed in the *Health Reports* you imply – you know sort of obliquely when you talk about the pill and the coil and sleeping with men who are promiscuous – you let your readers think that maybe they should think twice about me.

COSMO We want them to see you at your best, Sex. Don't you think it right that they should be aware of everything?

SEX I'm not exactly complaining. I'm very sensitive at the moment.

COSMO Why don't we go through your press cuttings? We see you've brought them in with you.

SEX Oh I'm going to need a stiff drink if we're going through these. I mean just look at them will you. '30,000 more suffer genital diseases'. That's terrible publicity. And look at this: '547,437 patients were treated for sexually transmitted diseases in National Health Service hospitals in 1983.' Who knows what they found in the private sector? Terrible. It's terrible. I didn't know where to put myself when *The Times* published that one. I didn't go out for weeks after that. Then there's this one about a Playboy bunny murdered by her husband. 'A tragedy of degraded sex,' they said in *The Mirror*. They blame me. Why didn't someone blame that crazy husband?

COSMO That's just sensational journalism. People always stop and read if you're mentioned in the headlines. You're always great copy. At least you're always being talked about. We're never unaware of you.

SEX Who wants to be talked about like that? Listen. That's all they're doing in some cases and I don't even get *talked* about in some households. Never even mentioned. Read this. 'No Sex please we'll

172

Sexclusive interview

settle for a cuddle.' I mean that's heartening. That's really heartening. They get married, they have kids and they don't want to know me any more. I'm out with the garbage. Tell me, do you watch a lot of TV?

COSMO Well, you know, we're busy people. But yes, sometimes. The news, documentaries, a good play. Maybe *Dallas*.

SEX My favourite. I'm on every week – you notice? But you know, *Dallas* apart, most of the programmes are lousy. There's nothing to watch. If it wasn't for JR I wouldn't even pay the licence fee. But what kills me, what really kills me is that most people – I'm talking of 92 per cent of people in this country – would rather watch lousy TV than have me around. Can you imagine they prefer TV to *me*? And the psychiatrist wonders why my self-esteem is in the basement.

COSMO Do you think some people don't understand you and therefore they're scared of you?

SEX Some people don't even know me. Look at this one. There's a wife who died a virgin after 24 years of marriage. Can you credit that?

COSMO Well some people can be happy without you, don't you agree?

SEX Sure. If they both want to visit the library together and they like being quiet and reading and not touching. Are you crazy? The woman in the press cutting left all her money to a cat's home. You can kid yourself all you like. I am in all the best marriages, all the best relationships. Love and me together. You've got to have both.

COSMO Can we see the other press cuttings you've got in your hand?

SEX I don't know if I can show you. I don't know if I can face your reaction. This has set me back light years.

COSMO We've come this far. Read it to us.

SEX You promise we're still talking after this? You'll still write about me once in a while? You know, a couple of lines at the end of the magazine. Anything. I don't expect a really big feature. You're decent respectable people. But you know, a tiny PS will do, just so long as you acknowledge me from time to time ...

COSMO We'll always acknowledge you. You know that. Come on. You're overreacting. It can't be that bad.

SEX It's that bad. OK, in for a penny. What more can I lose? Are you

Sexclusive interview

ready for this? It says, 'Warning! Avoid Sex in London.' There's someone from the Terence Higgins Trust saying 'AIDS is no longer a disease restricted to gay men. Anyone can get it,' Millions of people told to *avoid* me. I mean what kind of remark is that? They're making me synonymous with a killer disease. It's like saying, 'Don't fly, you'll crash.' Listen, I'm seeing my lawyer over that one.

COSMO Well, we did see the reports on AIDS in *Time* and *Newsweek*. It does seem fairly obvious that the healthy sexual style is the single partner. Of course, news reports such as these must make you feel very insecure. But it's confusing and worrying for us as well you know. We don't like the adverse publicity about any aspect of you any more than you do. Please understand, Sex, it's not that we don't like you, but obviously we've got to be cautious these days.

SEX You're telling me? I'm the one bearing the brunt of all this. People have always been confused about me. You think this is new? What's new? Every twenty years or so people change their minds about me. We want you, we don't want you, you're healthy, you're unhealthy, you're natural, you're unnatural. I'm having a breakdown trying to fathom out what people want. It's hell I tell you. I'm going nuts. Do you have any Kleenex in the office?

COSMO Don't get so upset. Oh please don't cry.

SEX No, leave me. Crying is good. I get it all out. I'll feel better afterwards. I may need some more tissues.

COSMO We didn't think of you as being emotional. Goodness, what a surprise. You're really rather vulnerable aren't you?

SEX Of course I'm vulnerable. You think you're talking to a rock? I've got feelings. I'm aware of atmosphere. Just because I brazen it out sometimes doesn't mean I don't notice what's going on.

COSMO What would you like in your ideal world?

SEX Nothing fancy. I don't have big social ambitions. You know me. I'll mix with anybody. Single, married, young, old, rich, poor. I don't care where people live. I'm not class conscious. I'd just like the human race to carry on. And I'd like a little fun and pleasure. It would be nice if people were happy to see me and not avoid me as if I'm a terrible person. I'd like more of the *little* things that thrill me.

Sexclusive interview

COSMO Give us an example.

SEX Well. Spending the weekend in bed with a nice couple. Anywhere will do. I'm not fussy. I wouldn't even object if they watch a little TV. Just as long as we're all there together enjoying ourselves. That makes me feel good.

COSMO You're right. There's not enough of those weekends any more. Maybe we'll run some articles on romantic weekends.

SEX A little romance would help. Oh, and they should find a cure for AIDS before I'm put out of business altogether. And I'd like more balanced reporting. When wonderful kids get born, somebody should say I had a hand in it. Credit where credit is due. You know, it would be good if more married people could be enthusiastic about me. What with multiple partners being a no-no – and believe me I understand how you're feeling – I'm having to rely on people with the *same* partner. Listen. Those marrieds are a big let-down. I'm there, ready for action and what do they do? Nothing is what they do. The statistics on when I'm not wanted after marriage would make your hair go limp.

COSMO Don't give them to us. The beauty department is right out of hair gel and we can't take any chances. You know we always suspected you weren't wanted too much after marriage. Maybe that's why so many of us stayed single. We'll think about that, Sex. We really will.

SEX I wish you would. It would be a big help for me in the future. You know the hardest part of these times for me? And if I'm honest, what's really depressing the hell out of me?

COSMO Be honest.

SEX You won't laugh?

COSMO Promise.

SEX You'll laugh.

COSMO You won't see as much as a faint smile on our lips. Tell us.

SEX I don't feel so sexy any more. I just don't feel sexy. That's just got to be the ultimate terrible situation. How could that happen to *me* of all people? Imagine.

COSMO We're not laughing. We're really not. We really don't mean to. Oh Sex, it's just such utter sweet relief that you feel the same way as we do. Thank goodness we spoke.

Whoops I'm single

*I*f marriage were a destination in a holiday brochure, eight out of ten clients would accuse the travel agent of misrepresentation. If it were a drug it would be withdrawn from the market because of the harmful side effects. If it were a nationally advertised product the makers would be prosecuted under the Trades Description Act. Yet marriage is regarded as the ultimate destination. Single is a state from which you are urged to emigrate on the SS *Relationship* even if it is a perilously frail craft. Single is seen as a journey to marriage, an *en route* stage. Useless to raise a small single voice and point out that to travel hopefully is sometimes better than to arrive.

Marriage is like a drug, in that most people seem to crave it in the hope that it will make life easier and more bearable. Single is sometimes seen as an unsocial illness – marriage will cure 'all that'. It's certainly advertised in a ceaseless lifelong campaign. The idea is sold to us via childhood fairy stories, books, plays, films, the media and our mothers. Married is better. The TV advertisements show married life as happy, secure, loving and ideal. The attractive blonde wife pours gravy over the Sunday lunch she's cooked for a rugged, adoring husband and two huggable children. The middle-aged couple, holding hands, are thrilled they took out an insurance policy together. A loving twosome fall asleep contentedly, assured they've chosen the perfect double mattress. Only the female dog breeders and cat lovers seem to live alone. Presumably with their animals to console them.

The intelligent single person knows full well that the mother of two could be heartily sick of cooking meals, the insurance buyers may well have spent boring, uneventful years together and the couple looking cosy on the shared bed stand a one in three chance of getting divorced.

Whoops I'm single

But the single girl, curled up alone on a wet weekend, isn't given to such cynicism. She *believes* what she sees. She buys the image she's being sold. Married is better. No one is selling single to her in such positive terms.

Society apparently sets little store by single. People don't say 'You're looking so well, single really suits you.' No one gives marvellous parties to celebrate 10 or 20 years of living alone. The best compliment it can pay to an attractive, charming, successful, single woman is, 'It's amazing that someone like you isn't married.'

Society, for its own ends, greatly exaggerates the plus factors of marriage and denies or ignores the positive aspects of living alone. Little wonder that many people marry with wholly unrealistic expectations about their partner and their happiness, and are sadly disappointed. Small surprise that even those who are happily single harbour the nagging conviction that somehow there's a better life to be lived.

And yet anyone can get married. Anyone does. It doesn't depend on great physical attraction or membership of Mensa. There are just as many dull married people as there are single people. So why do people remain single?

In many cases it's a matter of choice. It means a woman has been discriminating. She has refused to be brainwashed into marrying just anyone because it suits society's wishes. She has probably loved and felt the pain of loss. But if she's wise she knows that the most extraordinary love is not always made of the stuff that can be smuggled down the aisle or into a registry office. Like the best wine, it doesn't always travel the distance. She realises that 'I love you' is not invalidated because a marriage was not arranged. Some of the most passionate love affairs in history did not end in marriage. Some very mundane relationships do.

The single woman knows full well that she can experience the same degree of pleasure, excitement, caring, happiness, boredom, depression and loneliness as her married counterpart – if not more. Family life can inhibit the chances of good relationships outside the family. The single person is unfettered by such ties. She is free, she has choices. Could it be that single with its liberty and dazzling possibilities is *threatening*? Fortunately for society, most women do marry eventually. But isn't it

Whoops I'm single

time society admitted that single does have many advantages?

If you are single and living alone, you probably have far more personal living space than a married woman; you can arrange your home without having to consider anyone else's taste or convenience; you don't have to put up with anyone else's idiosyncrasies; you can sleep by yourself; you can sleep with a lover; you can choose your own friends; entertain whom you choose; you can cook when it suits you; you don't have to explain why you're going out or with whom; you can make spontaneous arrangements; you can spend your money as you wish; you can speak for as long as you like on the telephone; you can devote as much time as you want to your own well-being; you are never obliged to please anybody but yourself; you are free to demonstrate love and caring to a number of people.

It must be admitted that in addition to subtly discouraging single living, society actively penalises the single woman. Singles are more heavily taxed, have less chance of finding somewhere to live and very little chance of being offered government subsidised accommodation. Late-night shopping is a problem in many areas and hotels demand a supplement for single room occupancy. Married women can lack loyalty to their single women friends. And almost never is the single female executive invited home to dine with the wife and family of her male colleague; married men are very wary of introducing an unattached female, whether a friend or a co-worker, into their home environment.

Perhaps it takes more courage to be single. You must actively make plans, be assertive when you least feel like it, maintain the necessary self-discipline to get the best out of your life and at all times try to resist the temptation to lapse into singular apathy. Of course it's easier to go to the party or dinner party if you're Mrs Somebody. The married woman who finds herself standing alone with an empty glass can walk across the room to the safety of her husband. But it's a marvellously exhilarating feeling to know that you can enter a room without a partner, that you're capable of making a good conversation, that people like you and warm to you, that you can make it on your own. Of course it takes practice. But then living takes practice – it isn't simple for anyone!

But as more and more people are living alone, it must be remembered

Whoops I'm single

that single *never* needs defending. Nor should it be considered a problem in itself. Too many women take single far too seriously. Perhaps
they should remember, before they rush out to buy books on *How to
Survive Single*, that single seems to be more dangerously attractive to the
married than it ever does to the single woman. The married are mystified
and provoked by the independence of the unattached female.

Single does mean learning to live with yourself. But that's no more
difficult than learning to live with somebody else. Single means freedom.
You're free to see Paris on a May weekend, to take computer studies or
English Lit evening classes, to work late on an interesting project, to
spend the day in bed with a good book or a person who's read one. If the
single woman doesn't use her time properly she has only herself to
blame. Single means you have the time to grow and to be the person you
want to be. Single gives you space to grow. Sometimes it's harder to
grow when you're close to someone. Trees are planted far apart so that,
with the years, they can spread their branches and be strong and
properly balanced in their maturity.

Single means learning not to need a man to make your life work, but
being with a man because you want to be with him. Single means you're
not complacent. Single means that sometimes you'll wonder why
nobody can come out to play. Single means that sometimes you'll bite
your bottom lip and feel wistful and wonder if married is better. Happily
single is feeling good about controlling your life. It's liking and respect-
ing who you are and realising married is not better, it's just different.

Single means that there could be something wonderful around the
corner and you can take advantage of it. Single means you're free to fall
in love again.

Beachwatching

*S*omeone said that no-one was ever made unhappy in a brothel. It must have been a man. Jean Anouilh or Jean Genet? No he was a well-known gay person. Or do they have male brothels? Why don't I know about things like that? Maybe it was Cynthia Payne. Anyway, I was just sitting here, clasping my arms around my knees, feeling the grainy sand between my toes and thinking that no-one was ever made unhappy on a beach. I don't think I've ever been. Well, once, maybe. I love it in the early morning like this, when the sands stretch out and the beach is almost empty and the waves roll up with a gentle plllllaaaash on the shore, and those yellow beach umbrellas are lined up along the water's edge just waiting for their day to begin. My body is pale tan from yesterday which is an improvement on a couple of days ago when I looked like an aspirin. Honestly I can't believe this is bad for you. My face has come to life and my eyes look as though I'm enjoying myself. I really quite liked me in the mirror this morning. Oh the peace and utter contentment of sitting on a beach after an early swim, just to be able to sit here and gaze out to sea. There's a small sailboat coming around the bay with a man and a woman on board. He's bare torsoed with pale blue jeans and she's wearing a T-Shirt over her bikini bottom. They look so tanned and fit and happy. I feel I'm witnessing a perfect moment in their lives.

'You f------ c--- I *told* you to pull that f------ rope.'

'Don't you *dare* speak to me like that, you damn bully.'

'We are never, repeat f------ never, doing this again. I've had it.'

'Will you *keep* your voice down.'

Gosh. They seem to be having rather a problem struggling under those sails. And I always thought those little flotilla boats looked so easy

Beachwatching

and such fun. Doesn't the man sing 'True Love' while the woman rests her head in his lap and the boat just sails itself? Sometimes I misjudge situations.

Why have those people come running out with beach chairs and their own enormous umbrella? The beach is almost deserted. Do they have to stake out their territory *this* early? Oh come on. I think it's against the rules to yank up those two yellow umbrellas and stick them further up the beach and then plunge their hideous floral umbrella right near the sea. And a windbreak. Are they kidding? There's barely a breeze. Oh I love a stray dog. No, he can't be a stray. He's too boisterous and healthy looking. A cross between an Airedale and something I can't remember. Aaah! He wants to play with the woman with the blond lacquered hair and the white kaftan. He can't understand that he's found six people and none of them want to play with him because they're too busy putting up their chairs and spreading out their towels. Don't dogs race into the waves with such *gusto*? He's turning around now and dogging it back to the shore and yes, yes, he's shaking himself all over the white kaftan woman and she's furious. 'Get *away* you vile animal, get *away*' and I swear that dog is smiling as he capers off along the shore.

Funny that H never likes sitting on beaches. Paul was wonderful except for the sun block on his nose. But H seems to *inhale* a ruddy tan while Paul always had to try hard which infuriated him. Still he was the perfect beach companion. H can't sit still. Half an hour and he's restless and wants to *explore*. He does like boats though. He knows how to handle them and how to tie hundreds of useful knots and how to come alongside in style. Mind you, he's never even changed a *plug* at my place but maybe if I'd lived on a houseboat it would have been different.

Gosh, it's getting rather warm. I can really *feel* the sun on my arms and legs. Maybe I'll roll over and read *Professor of Desire* by Philip Roth. Desire ... I like that word. . . .

God. What time is it? Why do I always fall asleep in the sun? Why did I forget to take my bikini top off? Is there a silly white line across my back? Phew. It's hot, really hot. There's that rather nice woman I saw yesterday. How old would she be? Mid-thirties? I can't tell. She didn't look at all the type to go instantly topless. Funny how easy and natural it

Beachwatching

is for most women though. I forget that from year to year. What *is* her husband doing? I mean, what *is* that man doing? Oh God. The Englishman abroad. I mean there *she* is wearing practically nothing and putting down her knitting and helping her youngest son pull off his sweater and there's her husband struggling with his beach towel and trying to put on his swimsuit. And you'd think that everyone on the entire *beach* was deeply interested in *his* private parts. Whoops – he nearly lost his towel. Why are men so *obsessed* with their lower anatomy? So frantic with worry lest you should catch a *glimpse*? What a *relief* he's finally pulled his trunks on and now he's smacking his hands and trying to look masterful and saying who's for a swim. What kind of *sex* lives do those people have? I bet she spends a good deal of her life being disappointed. He must go to bed with those Y-fronts on and slide them off – please God he slides them off – as he slips coyly into bed beside her. Maybe he goes to bed first? There's the thing about coming away at the height of the season. You don't have the beach to yourself for very long. It's filling up now. There's that vast woman with the long brown hair piled on top of her head. She's lying face down with her flesh oozing over her black swimsuit. Her skin is going *very* pink. She really does look like a stranded whale. Mind you, it's quite *nice* flesh, it's just that there's so much of it. I wonder how people get to be that size? Well she's fast asleep and she doesn't look too worried about her weight problem. Should I suggest she puts some more cream on when she wakes? It's sad when you're on your own and you're not agile enough to rub cream on your back. I'll offer. Yes. And maybe I'll chat to her for a bit because I know what's it's like to be lonely.

Oh God. Here comes that girl with the most amazing body. She's probably called Maria. All those Page Three Girls are called Maria. That is *some* body. Does she exercise? I bet she doesn't. They never do. They just say they do. I'd have dark fantasies about her if I were a man. That T-Shirt which says 'Watch out dangerous curves' is just a teensy bit obvious. But er, yes, people are watching. Her girl-friend's not bad either. Blue-eyed blonds do look nice in the sun. As if they're born to be there. I'm not sure about the efficacy of those white sling back heels sinking into the sand. Perhaps they go out dancing immediately they

Beachwatching

leave the beach. The Italians have arrived. They must be Italian. They're so incredibly chic with their brilliantly coloured striped tops and that wonderful orange colour they seem to wear and they're so brown already. Oh. That one with the nice legs is called Pierangelo. I like that name. Pierangelo has spotted Maria with the amazing body and he's trying to pretend he hasn't seen her. His wife, I suppose it's his wife with the dark, straight shiny hair and the pale beige expensive looking shorts, probably wouldn't like Maria. Do Italians always travel in chic sets of three couples on holiday? And plan their co-ordinated wardrobes so they look like something out of Italian Vogue? Gosh, another Italian husband has spotted Maria, but no, he's been momentarily distracted by a troupe of Scandinavians looking like sunkissed angels. I wonder if they have *any* dyed blonds in Sweden. Swedish men don't seem to leap about looking for foreign women. Still I don't suppose I'd bother if I had such terrific home grown stuff. But, no, it's back to Maria who's settled in nicely now and she's arranged her navy and white beach towel and taken off the hat with the flowers and checked herself in the mirror and applied more red lipstick and yes, the bikini top is coming off. No-one is paying the slightest bit of attention now except for Pierangelo and his man friend who look dumbstruck at her D-cups and quite forget what they're supposed to be doing with the squishy portable beach freezer.

The yellow umbrellas by the sea have nearly all been claimed now and the rest of the beach is filling up in a companionable sort of way. Why do those two groups of people near the jetty get so cross if anybody wants to come by on their way to the water? Oh I like this georgeous couple jogging along in their short white shorts and smiling sideways at each other. No, I don't believe those jetty people won't let them jog past. That's ridiculous, having to make a detour around the deck chairs and umbrellas. Un-holiday spirited I call that. There's quite a few men with other men. *Not* the type to be interested in Maria. Gay men do seem to be in much better shape than most other men. Perhaps they have to try harder. I'm not sure about that couple with the G-Strings. Except those taut tanned bottoms do look rather, well, healthy I suppose. What do I think about gay men? I don't really grasp the concept. It's confusing. Men suddenly went from being much too interested in your physical

183

Beachwatching

attributes to not giving a damn if you lay around naked. Funny that. What happened to the men in the middle? Oh – there's a small thin man with a moustache and weedy legs who's very alone. I sort of hope he meets a prince. Now *this* couple are definitely in love. They're a matching pair with brown glossy hair and turquoise shorts and white beach bags and their arms around each other's waists. The cheeky umbrella man is chatting up Maria and her friend. Pierangelo is lying on his stomach next to his wife and peering at them over his black sunglasses. The Swedes look so good on their sailboards. Where do they practise in Stockholm? Isn't it a bit cold for that sort of thing there? I wonder what this beach looked like years ago when nobody came here. Before the tourists.

Those tall trees and pale stone houses have seen so many summers. So many scenarios played out on this long perfect strip of creamy white sand. The thin man with the weedy legs and the moustache gets points for boldness. He's asking the G-String Gods for the time. The time for what? Well, I must say they're friendly. He's wandered back to collect his skimpy towel and his small black roll of a beach bag and he's settled down next to them. Three's company. The matching glossy-haired lovers have run into the sea together. Now, what makes them think that no-one can see what they're doing? I mean even from here I can understand that what with him standing there grinning and her with her legs wrapped around him and throwing back her head and laughing, moaning, aqua sex is taking place. True the Italians are too busy pulling cold drinks out of their squishy freezer and the people by the jetty are now squabbling with each other about which small boy hit the other one first and most of the other people on the beach are stretched out sleepily in the heat. Sunsoaking one and all. Ah! *Some* people have noticed. The Swedes on the sand have just given the brown glossy-haired couple a cheer as they wade back to the shore. Lots of thumbs-up signs and now they're clapping and roaring their approval. And everyone has looked up wondering what the applause is about. The beached whale woman has woken up at last. Her face is creased from sleep and beads of perspiration are dripping down her forehead. I'm *sure* she's going to burn. Her back and legs are so red. I'll go over to her in a minute. Maria

Beachwatching

and her friend are oiling their bodies in a *very* provocative way. Will
Pierangelo and his friend be able to survive such tantalising? They're
looking at her open-mouthed over the tops of their glasses like children
aching for an ice-cream. A sudden gust of wind has uprooted Maria's
umbrella and blown it across the sand *thwack* into the G-String crowd.
Pierangelo is on his feet and running towards them. Our hero. There he
is gallantly dragging the yellow umbrella back to Maria and now he's
insisting there's a *special* way to twist the pole into the hot sand. Why do
his actions look so *sexual*?

The two girls look grateful in a bland sort of way. The blond says
'That's *reely* nice of you', and Pierangelo says 'Da niente' as he fervently
takes in what could be his only close-up of Maria's bouncing breasts.
Now *this* is what I call an attractive man. He's striding across the beach
and a few women sit up straight and one or two of them stroke their hair.
Well, maybe he's a touch on the heavy side but he has good legs and a
strong face with marvellous warm brown eyes and a terrific dimple on
the right side of his face. He's heading this way. He's looking around.
He glances at the G-Strings and Maria and then he sees who he's looking
for. He walks up to her and sits down next to her and tenderly strokes
her hair. The beached whale woman looks up from her prone position
and smiles at him. He tenderly creams her vast back, covering it with
white liquid, and then, slowly, gently rubs the back of her thighs. He
re-adjusts the umbrella to cover her from the burning sun, kisses the side
of her face, settles down next to her and I don't *believe* it, he too is
reading *Professor of Desire*. Maria slumps with disappointment and
decides to roll over and get her back brown. Pierangelo and his friend are
now staring at one of the Swedish girls who's changing out of her bikini
into a billowy see-through white cotton skirt and top, and she isn't
wearing underwear. Two of the Italian wives are gesticulating and
looking rather cross and Pierangelo and friend have had to turn their
backs on the underwearless Swedish blond and pretend that they'd
much rather play gin rummy. Oh. Who needs to read a book when
there's so much happening here?

Here comes H. With a friend. They both look wet and happy. Here's
H telling me he's found someone who *really* knows how to enjoy

Beachwatching

himself on the beach. And he pats the boisterous cross between an Airedale and something I can't remember and the dog leaps up and tries to lick his chin. What does he mean he doesn't know how I can spend hours on a beach doing nothing? What does he mean don't I get bored just lying in the sun? Why does he laugh and shake his head when I say I've been totally absorbed? I do love him. I just wished *he* loved beachwatching.